TANTRIC YOGA

AND
THE WISDOM
GODDESSES

Spiritual Secrets of Ayurveda

TANTRIC YOGA

AND
THE WISDOM
GODDESSES

Spiritual Secrets of Ayurveda

by David Frawley

Passage Press
Salt Lake City, Utah

Passage Press is a division of Morson Publishing
Morson Publishing
P.O. Box 21713
Salt Lake City, Utah 84121–0713

**This book is a reference work not intended to treat, diagnose of prescribe.
The Information contained herein is no way to be considered as a substitute for consultation with a duly licensed health-care professional.**

All translations from the Sanskrit by David Frawley
Cover design by Ted Nagata Graphic Design
Illustrations by Margo Gal

Printed on acid-free paper

ISBN 1-878423-17-7

May Uma, the Mother of the Universe with love, by the nectar of her moonlight smile, grant her grace to we who are afflicted by ignorance and pain.
— *Ganapati Muni, Uma Sahasram 1.1*

DEDICATION

To the great modern seer Kavyakantha Ganapati Muni, whose wealth of spiritual knowledge written in the most pure Sanskrit verses has hardly yet been touched — a Vedic, Vedantic and Tantric teacher and practitioner of the highest order.

May the publication of this book lead to a greater examination of his teachings and the ideas he set forth — the restoration of the full field of Vedic and Yogic knowledge, including Tantra.

To Ganapati's guru, Bhagavan Sri Ramana Maharshi, for as a true devotee the Muni would only speak of himself as Maharshi's disciple.

And to the Goddess whom Ganapati adored, the Divine Mother Uma, the bestower of Knowledge.

CONTENTS

— Contents —

LIST OF ILLUSTRATIONS

FOREWORD
by Georg Feuerstein, Ph.D.

Tantrism has a long and illustrious history in India, Tibet, Assam, Kashmir, and Nepal. Once widely celebrated, it acquired during the British Raj a notoriety that led to its suppression and almost complete disappearance in India. Today Tantrism is thriving only in the form of Tibetan Buddhism (Vajrayana).

One of the principal reasons for the decline of Hindu Tantrism was the inclusion of sexual practices in its rich repertoire, which offended the sensibilities of Hindu puritans. Although these practices were pursued by only a small Tantric minority, in the minds of the influential Hindu brahmins Tantrism and sexuality became almost synonymous.

A similar confusion exists nowadays in the West where Tantrism has been experiencing a moderate renaissance ever since the psychedelic revolution of the 1960s. Here, however, it is precisely the sexual orientation of Tantrism that attracts Western seekers who have tired of the sex-negative attitude prevailing in the Judeo-Christian tradition. Many Western seekers think of Tantrism solely in terms of its sexual practices, and not a few who actually immerse themselves in Tantric teachings do so merely for hedonistic reasons. Tantrism, however, is not about selfish pleasure but about ego-transcending bliss, and it is not about sex as such but about the transmutation of sexual energy.

Today we find ads for Tantra Yoga in a variety of publications, and those who happen to have their names on a New Age mailing list can expect to receive junk mail inviting them to Tantric celebrations in idyllic settings, promising pleasure and fun. This comeback, questionable though it is in some respects, represents a significant change from the 1920s when the first English translations of Tantric scriptures (called *Tantras*) were published . . . and largely ignored.

However, the recent increase in popularity has not gone hand in hand with a comparable deepening of understanding. This is most regrettable because Tantrism is a fascinating spiritual tradition that contains a wealth of insights useful to those who seek to explore the depths of human consciousness. Under appropriate guidance it can even be a potent tool of self-transformation and spiritual realization.

The problem is that few Western students of Tantrism go to the trouble of studying the Tantric literature itself (whether in the original Sanskrit language or in reliable translations). They also tend to overlook the fact that Tantrism is an initiatory tradition, that is to say, it is based on the time-honored guru-disciple relationship. No scripture can convey the living experience that is central to a spiritual tradition. It is the teacher's instructions that infuse the scriptures with lifeblood. Moreover, it is the guru who in countless practical ways assists the disciple's spiritual awakening and subsequent growth.

Tantrism is a powerful spiritual path, and like anything that is powerful it has its dangers. Without real guidance and a strong sense of responsibility, the Tantric practitioner is apt to succumb to ego-inflation and the misuse of the abilities awakened in him or her.

It is also true that few Westerners are prepared for a traditional pupilage. According to an old adage, the teacher comes when the pupil is ready. Clearly, then, anyone interested in practicing Tantrism must first study the Tantric teachings to obtain the necessary intellectual and moral foundation for real Tantric discipline. The present work by David Frawley (Vamadeva Shastri) is ideally suited to provide such a basis for further study and practice.

Tantric Yoga and the Wisdom Goddesses is an excellent introduction to the essence of Hindu Tantrism. The author discusses all the major concepts and offers valuable corrections for many existing misconceptions. He also introduces the reader to the core Tantric practices of meditation and *mantra* recitation, focusing on the Ten Wisdom Goddesses (*dasha-mahavidva*).

These Goddesses are personifications of the feminine aspect of the Divine. The Tantric practitioner approaches them and seeks to obtain their grace through ritual worship and meditation. The Goddesses' respective spiritual energies then convey the practitioner (*sadhaka*) safely and swiftly to Self-realization. The teaching of the Ten Wisdom Goddesses is little known but is characteristically Tantric, and it affords Western students reliable access to the metaphysics and spiritual discipline of Tantrism.

David Frawley is well known as a champion of Ayurveda (India's native medical tradition), Jyotisha (Indian astrology), and the *Vedas* (the earliest scriptures of Hinduism). In particular, his interpretations of the *Vedas* and his revisioning of early Indian history represent important contributions to a reappraisal of the spiritual wisdom originating with the seers and sages of India.

In the present book, David Frawley does for Tantrism what he has already done for the ancient Vedic tradition. He is a popularizer in the best sense of the word: He seeks to address as many readers as possible, endeavoring to communicate to them deep truths faithfully but without the overload of detail found in academic publications. While I do not always agree with him, I respect and appreciate his learning, understanding, and inspiration, as well as his passionate commitment to making India's wisdom accessible to Western seekers.

Anyone who has met David Frawley knows him to be a walking encyclopedia when it comes to Hindu metaphysics and spirituality. Knowledge bubbles forth from him like a clear, refreshing spring from which pilgrims can safely quench their thirst for higher wisdom. I can heartily recommend this work.

Georg Feuerstein, Ph.D., is the author of over twenty books, including *Encyclopedic Dictionary of Yoga, The Yoga-Sutra of Patanjali, Sacred Paths,* and *Wholeness or Transcendence?* He is on the editorial board of the *Encyclopedia of Hinduism,* a contributing editor of *Yoga Journal,* and senior editor of *Intuition magazine.*

Shri Ramana Maharshi and Ganaptai Muni

PREFACE

Tantra has become one of the more well known and popular aspects of Eastern spirituality in the world today. A whole modern neo-Tantra appears to be arising, with various forms in the Western world as well as in India. Tantra appears to have a freedom and universality that the modern mind is seeking, which is creative, diverse and stimulating and therefore wide in terms of its potential audience. Yet Tantra remains one of the least understood of the yogic teachings. The spiritual and meditational side of Tantra has not been explained in detail or in depth, particularly from the standpoint of the Hindu tradition, wherein perhaps the greatest diversity of Tantric teachings exists. Hence it is necessary that we take a new look at this important part of the Yoga tradition.

Tantra can perhaps best be defined as an energetic approach to the spiritual path, using various techniques including mantra, ritual, Pranayama, and meditation. It contains a devotional approach emphasizing the worship of the Goddess and her Lord, Shiva. It contains a way of knowledge, directing us to Self-realization and the realization of the Absolute. As such it is a complex yet integral system for the development of consciousness which has something for all those who are seeking the truth.

This book presents the meditational and mantric side of Tantra, which is the more common side of Tantra practiced in India. It is written from the standpoint of a practitioner and also from one trained in Ayurveda (yogic medicine). As such, it tries to present the living spirit and practice of Tantra, rather than just another academic view. The book is divided into three primary sections, with the fourth as an Appendix. The book attempts to present the background, theory, and practice of Tantric Yoga.

1. Part One examines the background of Tantra relative to modern culture, including Tantra in the West today, the traditional Hindu view of Tantra, and the different levels of Tantric teachings relative to the traditional understanding of Tantra in India. The purpose of this section is to create a foundation for the understanding of Tantra in its full scope.

2. Part Two presents one of the major teachings of Tantra — that of the Dasha Mahavidya or Ten Wisdom

Forms of the Goddess. All the levels of the Goddess from her symbolic forms to her higher meditational approaches are systematically explored. This is the core section of the book.

3. Part Three examines Tantric yogic practices specifically relative to Ayurveda, the traditional medicine of India. It gives detailed information about the process of the development of consciousness and the practices which help to facilitate it. This is the practical part of the book for yogic practitioners.

4. The Appendix correlates Hindu and Buddhist Tantric systems in one chapter, and includes a Sanskrit key, Sanskrit glossary, and bibliography.

Kavyakantha Ganapati Muni

Much of the Tantric knowledge presented here, particularly that relative to the Ten Wisdom Forms of the Goddess, is based upon the work of Kavyakantha Ganapati Muni (1878-1936). Ganapati was perhaps the foremost disciple of Ramana Maharshi, whom many regard as the foremost guru and sage of modern India. In fact it was Ganapati who gave Ramana Maharshi his name, as previously the boy sage was called Brahmana Swami. Ganapati and Ramana were regarded as modern incarnations of Ganesh and Skanda, the two children of Shiva and Parvati. I was blessed to receive nearly the whole mass of Ganapati's existent works through one of his few living disciples, K. Natesan, now in his eighties, who is their sole living repository. Nearly all these works are in Sanskrit, mainly in out of date editions or as copied by hand by Natesan from Ganapati's own hand written manuscripts.

Ganapati Muni was a great Tantric and wrote from his own experience. He was one of the greatest of all Sanskrit poets and understood the entire tradition, back to the oldest *Vedas*. He presented all the correlations of Tantra from outer ritual to the highest spiritual knowledge, and from its ancient Vedic roots. In his own life Ganapati had a unique yogic experience that indicates the extent of his realization. After years of intense yogic practice he experienced the opening up of his skull, the loosening of the suture at the top of the head. After that a light and energy radiated from the top of his head. He lived in the state transcending the ordinary mind-body complex, not just as an idea, but as a physical fact.

Ramana Maharshi

Ramana Maharshi (1879-1950) himself is well known as a jñani or silent sage and is not usually thought of as a Tantric teacher. However, he did install a Shri Chakra, the most important Tantric symbol, at his mother's Samadhi, which became the center around which his ashram has grown up. Both he and Ganapati Muni empowered the Chakra and observed the regular worship of it. When in the presence of Maharshi, Ganapati Muni was composing the concluding verses to *Uma Sahasram*, his great Tantric work on the Goddess, Maharshi opened his eyes and said, "Have you finished all that I have dictated?" In this regard we may consider that the Maharshi also had a place in the Tantric knowledge presented by Ganapati Muni.

Contact and study with other great Hindu gurus like Anandamaya Ma and Ramakrishna, the former the Goddess incarnate and the latter the great devotee of Kali, were also important inspirations in the search that has produced this book.

✳ ✳ ✳

There are two notable books that mention the Ten Wisdom Forms of the Goddess. The first is Haresh Johari's *Tools for Tantra*. It can be consulted for those who are looking for more information on the meditation forms and yantras for the Goddesses, the latter of which are given in color. The second is Shankarnarayanan's *The Ten Great Cosmic Powers*, which provides much information on the inner meaning of the Goddesses. Some of this derives from Ganapati Muni, as well as Sri Aurobindo. Shankaranarayan, like my friend and teacher M.P. Pandit, was a disciple of Kapali Shastri, who himself was the main disciple of Ganapati Muni and later joined Sri Aurobindo. M.P. Pandit, who passed away this year (1993) was an important source of inspiration for my Vedic and Tantric work, and also has some notable work on Tantra on his own.

Tantric Yoga and the Wisdom Goddesses is part of a series of books I have written on the greater Vedic (Hindu) tradition. Previous volumes deal with Ayurveda, Vedic Astrology, Vedic culture and its history, translations and interpretations from the *Vedas* and *Upanishads*, and studies in the Hindu Tradition. The present volume on Tantra fills in a major section of the tradition.

The book was not planned but happened spontaneously as a convergence of three factors. The first was my long term worship of the Goddess and her consort Lord Shiva. The second, as noted above, was my recent contact with the works of Ganapati Muni. The third factor was the growing interest in Tantra in the West and the need to inform people of the deeper meditational tradition of Tantra, which most people are not properly aware of.

Only through the grace of the Divine Mother (in her form of Rajarajeshvari or the Supreme Queen of the Universe) did the book take shape so quickly. The core of the book was written in February 1992, with revisions and additions through July, and some minor alterations after that point. The book is not based on any antecedent material of my own. However, a considerable amount of material originally part of the book explaining Hindu Tantra, Tantra and the Vedic and Vedantic traditions, Tantra and Astrology, and Tantra and other spiritual traditions throughout the world was not included so as to make the book simpler in its format. Perhaps I will make this additional material available in another form later should an interest in it arise.

The main person who helped inspire this book was K. Natesan, now staying at the Ramanasramam in South India, whose sole motivation has been to promote the teachings of his great guru Ganapati Muni. J. Jayaraman of the Ramanasramam also deserves mention for showing me how to chant many of the great hymns to the Goddess in Sanskrit through which my Tantric study has proceeded. Margo Gal did excellent work on the illustrations for the book, including all those for the Ten Wisdom forms of the Goddess, reflecting the highest traditions of South Indian art, and also produced them on a short notice. Ken Johnson was helpful with the book as usual examining and proofing the manuscript. The Thantra Vidya Peedham of Alwaye, Kerala, provided the illustrations for the chakras.

It is my fervent wish that this book will deepen the study of Tantra today and bring a respect for its meditational approaches. I also hope that it will help bring about an understanding of the close relationship between Tantra, Yoga, Veda and Ayurveda, which are different aspects of the same tradition, each inherent in the other, and perhaps the planet's most complete and integral system of spiritual development.

David Frawley (Vamadeva Shastri)
Santa Fe, New Mexico
July 1992

PART I

TANTRA RE-EXAMINED

The Goddess Speaks:

Before the beginning of the universe I alone existed, with nothing other than myself. That Self-nature is called by the names of consciousness, wisdom, and the supreme Brahman. — *Devi Gita IV.3*

I create the Father of the universe on the summit of the worlds. My origin is within the cosmic waters, in the universal sea. From there I extend to all the worlds and touch the ridge of Heaven.

I blow like the wind, setting in motion all the universe. Far beyond Heaven and beyond this Earth extends my greatness. — *Vak Ambhrini, Rig Veda X.125.7–8*

1
TRADITIONAL AND
MODERN TANTRA

Oh Goddess, Lord Shiva, having created the sixty-four Tantras to confuse the entire world to become dependent upon external powers, again by your word brought down your Tantra, which gives self-reliance and fulfills at once all the aims of life.
— *Shankaracharya, Saundarya Lahari 31*

In this section of the book we will examine the background of Tantra to help create a suitable foundation for approaching Tantra according to its deeper and higher practices. We will explore how Tantra relates to current cultural backgrounds and how Tantra has been understood from a traditional Hindu perspective. We will see that much of what is popularly believed about Tantra today is not correct, and learn about the many sides and dimensions of Tantra beyond current stereotypes about it.

MODERN TANTRA AND ITS MISCONCEPTIONS
Tantra is a complex tradition, interwoven with the spiritual teachings of India and beyond, going back far into ancient history. The popular understanding of Tantra in the West today represents only a part of this vast system of knowledge. Tantra in the West has come to be associated with special sexual practices, with the worship of the Goddess, with Kundalini and the chakras, with a life and body affirmative approach to the spiritual path, and with a temperament that is artistic and dramatic rather than ascetic and otherworldly. It is sometimes associated with all that is exotic, dramatic, or dangerous in spiritual practices. While there is some validity to this perception, it does not comprehend all the aspects of the Tantric tradition, nor reveal its essence.

We could compare the state of Tantra in the West with that of Yoga, with which it is related. Like Tantra, the physical side of Yoga is emphasized — the practice of yogic postures or asanas — even though these represent a small part of classical Yoga, whose main concern is meditation. We live in a materialistic age wherein spiritual traditions are recast or scaled down into a physical model. While this can be a helpful way of introducing teachings in today's cultural setting and certainly enriches our healing systems, it does not reveal the true scope or intention of these teachings.

TANTRA AND THE NEW AGE

Recent popular or New Age spirituality in America looks in many respects like a new form of Tantra, making use of both its occult and spiritual sides. New Age spirituality includes the exploration of a whole range of energetic practices via the body, senses and mind, both for achieving personal and spiritual goals, as well as a recognition of the Goddess. It appears to be an extension of Tantric openness and experimentation into the technological age.

Many of the new spiritual and occult teachings of this century in the West have a strong influence from Hinduism, Buddhism and Taoism — particularly the yogic traditions — and thereby show an influence of Tantra, which is an important aspect of these systems. Many are based on Theosophy and Alice Bailey, who borrow directly from Hindu and Buddhist teachings, including the *Vedas, Puranas,* and *Tantras.* Others use Native American paths which have much in common with Oriental teachings like Tantra. There is similarly an interest in Shamanism, whose ritualistic side resembles Tantra. In addition is a renewed interest in the older mystic traditions of Europe and the West — Christian mysticism, alchemy and astrology, Kabbala or Sufism — which appear to have more in common with Oriental teachings like Tantra than with their own orthodox counterparts. This trend includes a renewed interest in pagan European traditions, which have many affinities culturally and historically with the Vedic and the Tantric.

However, while there are many positive trends in this phenomenon, much more development is needed in order to make these new approaches into a serious tradition. We are still in the initial stages, exhibiting the creativity, confusion and chaos of a new birth. Not infrequently the more superficial, preliminary, or sensate side of these teachings are emphasized, with appeals to fantasy, self-indulgence and entertainment. The experiential and deeper spiritual side of the teachings is thereby misrepresented or missed altogether.

In addition, we have a syncretic predilection and like to combine various teachings and traditions together. This reflects the breaking down of barriers which is part of the global age that is beginning to dawn. While such open-mindedness is helpful in expanding our horizons, it is not without its limitations. Trying too quickly to combine spiritual teachings and traditions can be like trying to grow oranges, apples and bananas on the same tree — while it sounds like a good idea, it cannot work. A spiritual teaching develops organically and cannot be artificially combined with another, even with good intentions. A sampling or preliminary exploration of different teachings should not be equated with a real understanding growing out of serious practice. There may be any number of good spots to dig a well, but only if one digs deeply in a single place will one really find water — and only if one digs in a place where there *is* water.

Yet such difficulties should not invalidate the trend to return to an experiential form of spirituality, which is what is really motivating us toward yogic traditions, including Tantra. This movement must ultimately lead us to a comprehensive and global spiritual tradition that integrates ancient and Oriental spirituality into the modern world while purifying it of its cultural dross. Such a new tradition may not necessarily be called Tantra (and the name is not important), but it will have a strong Tantric element. However, some decades or even generations may be required for this new trend to be fashioned into a genuine tradition. To aid in its development a more serious and self-disciplined approach is required, and one that is based on a real understanding of the existing traditions.

TANTRA AND SEX

For most people in the Western world, Tantra means sex. Tantra is commonly associated with special sexual practices, different sexual postures, and sexual rituals. This does represent an aspect of Tantra and of Hindu thought, such as is found in the *Kama Sutra*, the Hindu manual of sexual love. While some Tantric teachings mention such practices, they are not necessary parts of nor the main focus of Tantric Yoga, which like all true yogic traditions, centers on mantra and meditation. Many Tantric texts contain no references to sexual practices. Others mention them as preliminaries or as only one possible line of approach. Yet others regard them as mere metaphors or symbols. The broad approach of Tantra contains ways to turn all ordinary activities — including breathing, eating and sleeping — into rituals or sacred actions, but this does not mean that Tantra is promoting such activities for ordinary gratification.

Though Tantra does contain sexual Yogas, it is wrong to think that Tantra is characterized by them. In the same light Tantric art, which has an erotic appearance, is meant as a depiction of the higher forces of consciousness through which the primal forces of life can be transformed. It is not a glorification of ordinary sexuality, though it is unafraid of this force and is able to see the cosmic power working behind it.

Non-Sexual Tantra

Tantric teachings are an integral part of the monastic and ascetic traditions of India. There is a strong Tantric side to the Vedantic Swami orders, which involves the worship of the Goddess and the Shri Yantra. Most Hindu ashrams and monasteries conduct regular forms of Tantric worship. Shankaracharya (c. 500 AD), the founder of the Vedantic monastic orders, was himself a great Tantric adept, yogi and devotee of the Goddess, though he was also a sage and philosopher of the Absolute.

In India a Tantric master usually means a person who is a master of mantra or an energetic type of Yoga practice and does not connote one who is adept at sexual practices. Great Tantric teachers include figures like Shankara, Ramakrishna, and Nityananda, who were life-long celibates.

Yet this does not mean that one has to be celibate to benefit from Tantra. Tantra is not characterized by sexuality or its negation, but by various energetic approaches like mantra and yantra which can be applied on many levels and which provide tools for people of all temperaments and capacities. Tantra emphasizes methodologies of transforming energies and is not concerned with either suppression or ordinary indulgence through which energy is dissipated.

Sexuality and Liberation

The spiritual traditions of India — whether Hindu, Buddhist, or Jain — emphasize transmuting sexual energy because sex is the core energy of our existence. This has created two approaches. The first is a renunciate tradition in which all sexual activity is voluntarily given up. The second is a householder tradition in which moderation in sexuality is practiced.

The householder tradition may include sexual yoga practices, though seldom the graphic kind depicted in modern Western books on Tantra. It also aims at sustaining the social order through the family system, and thereby emphasizes sexual purity and loyalty. While the renunciant tradition is generally thought to be more direct because it allows the aspirant to focus entirely on practice, this is only a general rule. Many great yogis have come from householder traditions, and many Vedic rishis were married and had children. According to the Hindu tradition, human beings can live a householder life and fulfill their social and family duties and still achieve liberation.

While the renunciant tradition is generally more direct, it is more strenuous, and is the exception rather than the rule in all times and cultures, even those eras which are enlightened. It is a particularly difficult path in the modern age and in the Western world where there is no cultural tradition to support it. In this regard Yoga never encourages us to merely repress ourselves, though it does encourage self-discipline and says that we never need to bow down to the forces of desire. Yoga is part of an organic process of higher evolution whereby we naturally come to transcend our outer limitations into a state of inner freedom and contentment. It does not tell us that we must give up what provides us with happiness, but suggests that we should consider where our real happiness comes from. True happiness resides in consciousness, not in any material form, identity, or activity.

The Yoga tradition does not reject sexual energy as evil, bad, or shameful. Celibacy is only recommended along with spiritual practices to transmute that energy for usage on another level. Without meditation practices the Yoga tradition considers that celibacy may be harmful because the unused energy can stagnate and cause various physical and emotional problems. Yet without some control of sexual energy there will not be the power necessary to do higher meditation practices.

TANTRA AND THE BODY

Tantra affirms the importance of the body as a temple for the Divine and grants it a sacred reality. It views our psycho-physical organism as a microcosm in which the individual soul can understand the workings of the entire universe. For this reason Tantra has been regarded as a body-affirmative form of spiritual tradition, as opposed to teachings which negate the body. However Tantra does not affirm ordinary bodily identity, but sees the body as a mystic symbol. Yoga and Vedanta, which have been criticized as being against the body or anti-life, do not condemn the body either; they only negate attachment to the body and the sense of bodily identity (the I-am-the-body idea). Yoga looks upon the body as a temple for the Divine and as a mirror of the universe. On the other hand, ordinary people who affirm the body as the means to ultimate happiness end up abusing the body in order to achieve pleasures that are never really fulfilling anyway.

The body is the best vehicle nature can provide to aid us in our spiritual growth and is a great symbol for the different levels and powers of the cosmos. However, the body is not our true Self. The body is subject to disease, decay and death and cannot possibly provide lasting happiness, which can never be found in anything transient. However marvelous a vehicle the body may be and however much we can learn from it, there is no more bodily fulfillment than there is fulfillment for our automobile, which like the body is an instrument of experience but not our true identity.

We should respect the body and care for it properly because it is our means of gaining experience and enlightenment. Without energy and sensitivity in the body we cannot go far on the spiritual path. There is a natural intelligence in the body that shows us how to use it in the right way. This intelligence, which is part of the cosmic mind, reveals itself when we no longer use the body to pursue personal desires but as an instrument of developing higher awareness. The truth is that we are inherently happy and free as conscious beings, even without a body. Supreme happiness lies in being who we really are, which is not mere flesh but pure awareness. Hence the idea that Tantra is body-affirmative can be misleading and should be understood only in the sense that Tantra regards the body as a sacred ground for the Divine Self to be realized.

TANTRA AND THE REALITY OF THE WORLD

Along with the idea that Tantra is body-affirmative is the idea that Tantra is world-affirmative and Tantric philosophy grants a reality to the external world which is not found in other systems. According to this view there is an inherent opposition between Tantra and systems that negate the world (and the body) as unreal. Some Tantric teachings do give more reality to the world of manifestation than the Mayavadic or illusionist view of non-dualistic (Advaita) Vedanta, which states that the world is unreal and God is the only reality. Typical in this respect is Kashmir Shaivism. However, the Tantric systems which affirm the reality of the world, affirm its reality as consciousness and are quite removed from modern materialistic conceptions.

Contrary to this view of Tantra as world-affirmative, we should note that the predominant form of Tantra in India today — the worship of the Goddess through the Shri Chakra — is generally presented from the perspective of non-dualistic Vedanta. Many great proponents of world-negating Vedanta have been Tantric masters. Most notable is Shankaracharya, the greatest of the Vedantic philosophers, who wrote many famous Tantric works on the worship of the Divine Mother (like *Saundarya Lahiri*).

The Shakta tradition itself (the tradition that worships the Goddess or Shakti) is generally Advaitic and Mayavadic and asserts that the world is unreal. The *Devi Bhagavata Purana*, one of the most important Tantric works on the worship of the Goddess, gives such a teaching. This is unlike the *Srimad Bhagavatam* of the Vaishnavis (worshippers of Vishnu), which follows a dualistic (dvaita) view of creation. As Vaishnava teachings grant reality to the outer world, we can see that this view has never been regarded as the sole property of Tantra.

There is nothing in Tantra which is inherently opposed to world-negation approaches, nor is there anything in world-negation approaches that is inherently opposed to Tantra. There is not only a strong Tantric tradition of world affirmation, there is also a strong Tantric tradition of world negation. In the world-negation traditions the Goddess herself is worshipped as the Supreme Self or Absolute beyond all manifestation.

TANTRA AND EMOTIONS

There is a trend today, particularly in psychological circles, to emphasize the value of expressing emotions or reliving powerful emotional experiences and traumas. This is to counter a cultural tendency to suppress emotions and to deny our feelings. Tantra looks upon emotions as tools for spiritual growth. Hence Tantra has been regarded as affirming the validity of emotions, as compared with traditional spiritual teachings which negate emotion.

However, traditional Tantra does not encourage mere emotional expression, which only causes greater attachment to emotions and through them to the outer world. Tantra regards emotions as trapped energy and seeks the release of that energy, in which the form of the emotion subsides like a wave into the sea of awareness. This process occurs when we recognize that emotions are various cosmic energies limited and broken up by patterns of attachment. Tantra uses forms of the Gods and Goddesses — like peaceful or wrathful deities — to help us contact the cosmic meaning of emotion, which is just a force of nature. Seeing the Divine energy, or play of consciousness, inherent in emotion, we discover emotion as a means of relating to the Divine within us. While Tantra does not deny emotion, it should not be associated with mere emotionalism but with the alchemy of transmuting human emotions into Divine energies through developing devotion. Tantra does not emphasize the personal expression of emotions but the understanding of emotion as a play of consciousness.

Nor do traditional or so-called ascetic yogic approaches simply suppress or deny emotion or any other force of nature, which cannot be a means of liberation for anyone. It is not emotion or any aspect of energy in itself that Yoga seeks to negate but the ego, which is the selfish appropriation, and therefore abuse, of the beneficent energies of life. Yoga does not encourage suppressing anything that is natural to us, but discovering our true nature in which we can naturally let go of all attachments and dependencies.

TANTRA AND THE USE OF INTOXICANTS

Those who use psychedelics or mind-altering drugs have claimed some affinity with Tantra, where the use of intoxicants sometimes occurs. Like the sexual practices, Tantric teachings regard the use of intoxicants as a preliminary step or as a metaphor — wine for example signifying the inner flow of bliss released by the practice of Yoga. The use of intoxicants is found in Tantra but is also not characteristic of it. There has been some use of marijuana (ganja) by Indian sadhus outside the Tantric tradition as well, but most teachers do not encourage this.

While psychedelic drugs take us out of ordinary consciousness and may help open our horizons in life, their ability to do so is limited and to use them repeatedly must have side-effects. There are ways to do this which are safer, more beneficial and long-term ways to do this, as in the mantric and meditational practices of the primary yogic path.

TANTRA AND CRAZY GURUS

Tantric gurus, particularly in this country, have a reputation for acting in an unconventional, dramatic or even contradictory manner, which sometimes includes entering into sexual relationships with disciples, or acting toward them in an abusive manner. Tantra, with its open view of things, is more tolerant of such exceptional behavior, and some Tantric teachings say that these methods can, under certain circumstances, be helpful in shocking a disciple into awakening.

Yet such unconventional behavior can be used as an excuse to cover an inability to control our desires, and can result in exploitation. We should note that many Tantric gurus have been figures of the most exemplary conduct, and unusual behavior is not a necessary prerequisite of Tantric teachers. This does not mean that a true teacher cannot act in an unconventional manner or that he or she must cater to the disciple's preconceptions, but that being a teacher should require a higher, not a lower standard of behavior than that of ordinary people. Being a spiritual teacher should not be a license to do what one wants but an example for others to follow. Hence crazy gurus or crazy wisdom is not the essence of Tantra, though it has a niche within Tantric history.

We should also note that some of the teachers who have become famous in the West as Tantric or crazy gurus have not themselves come from any real traditional background, and have been self-proclaimed gurus, without having had any real guru of their own.

Not surprisingly, Tantra does have a bad reputation in a number of spiritual circles. This is largely owing to the excesses of Tantra which can include unusual sexual practices, intoxicants, magical practices to inflict harm or take control of other people, and other methods considered to be impure. For this reason many teachers — including some who have been true Tantric teachers — have avoided using the name Tantra. They may prefer to emphasize Vedic, Yogic or Vedantic traditions that include Tantra but are not tarnished by its misconceptions. Swami Vivekananda himself — the first major figure to bring Yoga and Vedanta to the West a hundred years ago — was careful to avoid introducing Tantric concepts to Western audiences, though he was familiar with them from his own teacher Ramakrishna, who was a Tantric adept. This was not only to avoid offending the Victorian mind, but to avoid appealing to the sensate side of the modern mind, which was also in evidence in his time.

TANTRA AND THE WORSHIP OF THE GODDESS

Tantra is associated with the worship of the Goddess, the feminine aspect of Divinity, and this is one of its prime features. Tantra provides a whole spiritual science for the worship of the Divine Mother, not merely a set of beliefs or dogmas but a practical way of developing our higher awareness through Her wisdom and Her grace. For those seeking to understand the religion of the Divine Mother, Hindu Tantra is perhaps the best key.

Yet there are also Tantric teachings which focus on Shiva, Vishnu and other Gods and in which the Goddess does not play a central role. Tantra is not limited to Goddess worship, and some form of Goddess worship is found in all the traditions of India going back to the most ancient Vedic. It is not unique to the Tantric.

Traditional Tantra gives reverence to both male and female powers and affirms that the God and Goddess go together, support each other, and should be worshipped together. Along with the Goddess is her consort, the great God, Lord Shiva. Their children — Ganesh and Skanda — play an important part, as do the deities of the Hindu pantheon, which are all related to each other.

Sex and the Goddess

Traditional Tantra gives reverence to the Cosmic Feminine in all her forms up to pure consciousness itself, which has feminine qualities of receptivity, loving kindness and compassion. Tantra views the feminine as the embodiment of wisdom and the energy of consciousness, and the masculine force as being, will and perception.

The Goddess possesses all forms of beauty, including that of the world of Nature, up to the highest beauty, which is pure consciousness. In fact wherever there is beauty in form it is only owing to its pervasion by some quality of the Goddess. Nature herself, with the beauty of the flowers, forests, mountains, ocean, and sky is the dance of the Goddess. While sexual beauty is one aspect of her delight — and that most evident in the human world — the purpose of Tantra is into bring us in contact with the reality of the Goddess directly within ourselves, whereby we can experience her ultimate beauty in our own minds. The Goddess is much more than sexuality, though sexuality can be used as a metaphor for her qualities. The Goddess is the bliss of Being, and we can never be content unless we realize this joy within our own hearts.

TANTRA AND KUNDALINI

Kundalini, often translated as the "serpent power," is a term which has gained some recognition today, particularly in yogic and New Age circles, though it is seldom properly understood. Kundalini literally means a coiled-up energy or the power that dwells in a cave (kunda). For any transformation to be possible, an energy is needed to bring it about. For the transformation of consciousness a special and powerful energy is needed. This is Kundalini.

Tantra presents a whole yogic and mantric science for developing Kundalini. However, this Tantric science has its foundation or parallels in Vedic, Vedantic and Yoga texts that speak of the transforming word (vak), the energy of consciousness (chit-shakti), or the power of knowledge (jnana-shakti), which are all synonyms for Kundalini.

The traditional role of Kundalini is different than the way in which it is generally viewed today, which is to regard it as a mere force to control and harness. Kundalini is a form of the Goddess and should be worshipped as Her power. It is not some psychic energy to be aroused but a Divine energy to be revered. Efforts to manipulate Kundalini through willful practice or forceful techniques are not only dangerous, but fail to recognize the reality of the Goddess and are contrary to her worship.

Many yogis, including Tantrics, may use no specific practices or Pranic manipulations to arouse the Kundalini. The arousing of the Kundalini can occur through intense devotion or profound meditation and does not require the use of specific Yoga techniques. Higher direct realization or knowledge approaches may not even mention the term Kundalini. Energy always follows consciousness and does not have to be approached as an end in itself. On the other hand, if we pursue energy apart from consciousness we may gain power, but, as it is not under the control of awareness, it is likely to have undesirable side-effects.

When Yoga techniques are used to arouse the Kundalini — and they are often very helpful — they should be done as part of a practice of surrender to the Divine or inquiry into the Self-nature. Without this basis they cannot be done correctly. The yoga student should first have a background in meditation, control of the senses, and an understanding of the workings of the mind before trying to arouse the Kundalini.

TANTRA AND ART

Tantra is allied with all forms of art in India. As the Goddess is the Divine Word, Tantra is closely associated with the tradition of Sanskrit poetry, and the entire tradition of Sanskrit learning and literature has a strong Tantric imprint. Stories of Shiva and Devi (the Goddess), popular in Tantric teachings, are the basis of Indian music and dance. Shiva is known as Nataraj or the Lord of the Dance. The Goddess has her own special gentle dance called the lasya. Indian art, including painting, sculpture and architecture, has a basis in Hindu mythology which Tantra shares. The many images and statues found in Hindu temples are fashioned and worshipped according to the rules prescribed in Tantric texts.

Today we need to recreate a more dharma-oriented artistic tradition and bring back the use of the image, icon and a way of sacred art. Tantric art can show us how to do this. But the artistic side of Tantra has its discipline. It is not a tradition without rules, or one that approves of anything dramatic, sensational, novel or unconventional as art. Tantra provides a structured and orderly conception of art based upon an understanding of the occult and spiritual laws of the universe.

TANTRA AND SCIENCE

Tantra is a kind of science, a way of knowledge both for understanding the outer world and the inner psyche. Tantra is based on and closely allied with the various traditional sciences of India, of which the two most notable are Ayurveda (Vedic medicine) and astrology (Jyotish). In addition some modern scientists find the energetic concepts of Tantra to be similar to their own discoveries.

Tantra is allied with the alchemical traditions found throughout the medieval world, including China, India, the Middle East and Europe. In fact, much of what has been called alchemy is simply Tantra as a global tradition. In this regard Tantra is nothing new, but the revival of the old alchemical and hermetic approach which is the basis of much of European mysticism.

The alchemical tradition exists within contemporary Ayurveda, which uses special preparations or alchemical forms of sulphur, mercury, mica, and other minerals. Ayurveda uses Tantric practices as part of its treatment for mental health, as well as for rejuvenation. Both Tantra and

Ayurveda are becoming popular in the modern world; their connections will be discussed in the third section of this book.

Tantric practices are timed according to the rules of Hindu astrology. Symbolism based on Hindu astrology occurs in many Tantric teachings. Tantric methods — including rituals, mantras and gems — are also used for balancing planetary influences as part of astrology. Hindu astrology includes palmistry and other forms of divination, many of which came to Europe along with the gypsies, who originated in India. These are also part of Tantric science which seeks to unlock the underlying laws of life.

Tantric science thus includes spiritual, occult and material sciences and is a possible model for the holistic science that the coming global age demands.

TRADITIONAL HINDU TANTRA

Hindu Tantra is a complex system of spiritual knowledge, an integral part of Hindu spirituality and the traditions of the Himalayan region. Yet Hinduism is not a religion in Western sense of a belief-oriented system emphasizing one book, prophet or church. Hinduism is not an exclusive belief which says that other religions are false, but an open spiritual tradition that accepts all useful practices and insights and which encourages diversity, innovation and individual freedom. The correct name for Hinduism is Sanatana Dharma, which means the "eternal truth or law," referring to a teaching not based on a particular savior, scripture, or historical revelation but a living unfoldment of eternal truth relative to constantly changing human conditions.

Hindu Tantra, like the Hindu tradition itself, contains many teachings, including some which are variant, alternative, or apparently contradictory. What is said briefly to characterize the tradition may only be true of one aspect of it. To really understand it we must examine its teaching as a whole. The Hindu tradition contains a multidimensional approach which includes different teachings for various temperaments and different levels of seekers. There are many different teachers, names and forms of the Divine, and yogic paths that one can choose from. Hence we must not jump to conclusions. The tradition is like the proverbial elephant, and we are the blind men who identify the whole animal with the one part their hands can touch. What may appear to be contradictory teachings are different parts of the same profound system of knowledge.

The Hindu tradition has often been criticized as being too formless, impersonal and otherworldly, seeing the world as illusion or Maya and the Absolute as the real truth. On the other hand, it has also been criticized for recognizing every conceivable form and personal expression of the

Divine — which is a criticism of the opposite nature. Hinduism not only has the idea of the formless immutable Brahman, but also the image of baby Krishna, the erotic forms of the Goddess, Hanuman with the form of a monkey, and Ganesh with an elephant face. Hinduism is not only the most ascetic or otherworldly of religions with its yogis and forest renunciants, it is also the most life-affirming, filled with stories of love, marriage and family life, like the stories of Rama and Krishna. There is no contradiction between these two sides, for Hinduism emphasizes transcending life through understanding it, not merely through denying or suppressing it.

The Meaning of the Term Tantra

In the most basic sense the Sanskrit term Tantra means merely nothing more than a "book." Any number of books on any number of subjects can be called Tantras. More specifically Tantra means a practical book — one that contains information and techniques — though it may contain philosophy as well. Tantra primarily means a compendium of various sorts of spiritual and occult knowledge, particularly those dating from medieval times in India. The term Tantra first appears about two thousand years ago and becomes prominent in teachings over the last 1500 years. There are not only Hindu Tantras but also Jain and Buddhist Tantras. There are not only Tantric teachings for liberation but for the ordinary goals of life. There are not only spiritual Tantras but those for almost any field of human knowledge. Yet Tantric texts do have certain general characteristics.

Tantra and the Hindu Tradition

In the Hindu tradition, teachings are of three orders:

1. Vedic
2. Puranic
3. Tantric

This division is largely one of time. The oldest level is the Vedic, then the Puranic, with the Tantric being the more recent formulation of the teaching.

The *Vedas* derive from the ancient Sarasvati river culture that flourished in North India between the Yamuna and Indus rivers before 1900 BC. This civilization is more commonly known as the "Indus Valley culture" or "Mohenjodaro and Harappa," after its first two large cities discovered. It is now known to have been centered on the Sarasvati river of Vedic fame, and is being more appropriately renamed the "Sarasvati Culture."

The *Puranas* reflect a shift that occurred when the center of Indian civilization moved to the Ganges-Yamuna plain after the Sarasvati river went dry (around 1900 BC). The *Tantras* derived from the Puranic teachings, largely in medieval times, and are based on Puranic myths and deities. While all three layers of the teaching have much in common, there is a shift in language and forms, as is natural in the course of time.

Yet we should note that Vedanta — which deals with the unity of the individual Self with the supreme Godhead — has persisted together with both Puranic and Tantric approaches and represents the essence of the *Vedas* as well. It is the constant element in the tradition.

Characteristics of Tantric Texts

Traditional Tantric texts are said to relate to the five following topics:

1. Creation of the universe
2. Destruction of the universe
3. Worship of the Divine in various forms
4. Attainment of the goals of life and spiritual powers
5. Ways of meditation to realize the ultimate truth

Tantras contain teachings dealing with the whole spectrum of human concerns; for the stages of life from youth to old age, for the different classes of society, rituals for public welfare including acts of charity, rules for temple worship, sacraments of various kinds and, most importantly, Yoga practices. Tantras are manuals for the entire community. A typical text in this regard is the *Mahanirvana Tantra*. The Tantras are broad texts and not specialized in any particular direction. If we examine the bulk of Hindu Tantric lore, we see that it possesses the following characteristics:

1. Tantra emphasizes techniques or energetic approaches, including ritual, mantra and visualization, though these are generally employed as a means to take us ultimately beyond techniques, rather than as an end in themselves.

2. Tantra has a universal approach that uses all available methods and rejects nothing. It includes methods that may be rejected in other teachings as "unspiritual."

3. Tantra gives a special place to the Goddess and her worship.

Lesser and smaller Tantric texts deal with specialized topics within these fields. Some are purely spiritual in nature and give secret keys to meditation and the chakras. These are probably the most interesting Tantric works. Other are mundane, dealing with science, astrology or similar topics. Yet others deal with occult and magical practices, including what could be called black magic — harming, paralyzing hypnotizing others, or placing them under the control of one's will. However, these lesser Tantras — which are the most sensational and have drawn the most attention — should not be thought of as representing the higher truth of Tantra or its ultimate goal.

FOR THE FUTURE

Tantra as a tradition, both in the Western world and globally, is here to stay. Its broadness and diversity will continue to support it. But Tantra has developed to a stage wherein we must approach it at a deeper level. This requires clearing away limited understandings of Tantra and going beyond the naive view of Tantra as mere sex and sensation. We must now recognize the full scope of Tantra with its many dimensions of spiritual, occult, artistic and scientific knowledge.

2
TANTRIC
PATHS

Those who use wine and flesh to worship you, Goddess who are the life of Shiva, have no fault, but those who are attached to these substances have their worship spoiled.

The devotee attains success by the right-handed path, the hero by the left-handed path. The silent yogi attains success by the celestial path, neither to the right nor the left.

On this most blessed celestial path, he does not carry the burden of worship, or the recitation of mantras. With a silent mind one should continually search for the supreme lotus feet of the Mother.

— Ganapati Muni, Uma Sahasram 17, 22–3

Yogic traditions, usually contain two paths:

PATH OF DIRECT AWARENESS — formless meditational approaches for direct realization

PATH OF TECHNIQUE — whether meditational or ritualistic, for gradual realization

Tantra is primarily a form of the second or gradual path. The first is represented in the Hindu tradition mainly by Advaita or non-dualist Vedanta, which aims at the direct realization of the Self as Absolute (Brahman). Buddhist direct paths include Chan and Zen, and Tibetan Dzog Chen, and the Taoists have such practices as well.

However, these two paths are not rigidly divided from one another and are integral parts of the same tradition. Tantra contains, as its higher teachings, direct approaches along the same lines as non-dualistic Vedanta, aiming at immediate Self-realization. Direct approaches also contain, as preliminary or support teachings, the use of techniques. The direct approach is best if we are truly capable of it, but it requires a high level of spiritual maturity.

UMA PARVATI

While techniques have their limitations in that they are bound to the realm of form, they are practical and present methods that can be applied even at the level of a beginner. It is not always possible to silence the mind directly, but it is always possible to repeat a mantra. While we may become attached to the mechanical repetition of techniques, we may also become caught in a purely speculative involvement with "direct" teachings. We may get trapped in the idea of direct awareness when it may be more useful for us to practice a mantra or other technique. Hence there is constant interplay and balance necessary between the two sides of the path as technique and realization.

If one can go immediately to the direct realization then naturally there is no need for techniques. If, however, one cannot go directly to it or cannot abide in it — which is the experience of almost everyone — then techniques can be beneficial. Even if one can abide in direct awareness, the use of techniques like Pranayama may still be useful to give one increased health and vitality. Techniques have benefits for the body and mind that should not be underestimated even if one recognizes their limitations in bringing about direct realization.

RIGHT AND LEFT-HANDED TANTRA

Tantra is most commonly divided into two paths:

1. Right-handed Path, Dakshinachara
2. Left-handed Path, Vamachara

The right-handed path emphasizes meditational and spiritual disciplines and insists on a high degree of purity in conduct and action. The left-handed path employs various sexual practices or the use of meat and intoxicants which are not approved along the right-handed path.

The right-handed and left-handed paths relate to the two main Tantric lineages, the Samaya and the Kaula. Samaya means "according to the rule," which refers to following strict dharmic principles. Kaula means "relating to Kula" or "according to the family," meaning that it allows local variations. However the Kaula path also mainly follows meditational approaches, and it would be wrong to equate it with what is commonly thought of as left-handed Tantra.

The right-handed path is said to be for "bhaktas" or those of devotional temperament. The left-handed path is said to be for "viras" or those of strong or heroic temperament, which refers to the warrior class (kshatriya). The right-handed approach can be called the orthodox path, or that of those who follow the prescribed rules of conduct, whether for the Hindu social dharma or for yogic practices. The left-handed path allows unorthodox practices which may be outside both the Hindu social dharma and the usual rules of yogic practices. Yet the Kaula path also contains much in it that is part of the Hindu tradition as a whole and is an integral part of it. Buddhist Tantra is based on the Samaya or right-handed tradition.

The right-handed path consists of mantra, Yoga and meditation. Rituals are secondary to it or used only symbolically. It is this tradition that is most common in monastic or Brahmanical circles. Monks renounce their social position and for them ritual, which in Hinduism is generally for the ordinary sacraments of life like marriage, is not necessary. The left-handed path has accepted within itself factors rejected by the right-handed path. But it does not consist entirely of these. The left-handed path may merely refer to an emphasis on the Goddess, who is the left side (vama) of the deity, and does not necessarily involve unorthodox practices.

Another distinction is that the left-handed path is said to be the way of ecstasy and the right-handed path the way of peace. Along the way of ecstasy we may be inclined to certain extreme actions as we break through preconceptions and as deep internal energies are released. Yet it is only peace that is lasting. In this chapter we will examine the philosophy and practice of the left-handed path because the main section of this book is devoted to the right-handed path.

The Five Forbidden Things

Left-handed Tantra prescribes use of the five forbidden things. They are also called the five "M-s" or "Makaras." They are:

1. Maithuna, sexual union
2. Mada, wine (and other intoxicants)
3. Mamsa, meat
4. Matsya, fish
5. Mudra, parched grains (or money)

Partaking of these items is forbidden or restricted in the codes of conduct followed by most Yoga traditions in India, as such things are considered to have a long term tamasic or dulling effect upon the mind. Hence it is clear that their usage is part of an exceptional path. In Tantra these items are offered to the deity as part of worship. Tantra, even of the left-handed path, does not recommend their ordinary usage for self-enjoyment. While these substances are not pure, the act of offering them to the deity purifies them and allows them to aid in spiritual growth.

Left-handed Tantra is itself divided into two traditions, the "symbolic" versus the "literal" tradition, depending on whether the forbidden substances partaken of are actually physical or mere metaphors.

The Symbolic Tradition

The symbolic tradition uses the five forbidden things only as symbols. Intercourse is the union of Shiva and Shakti, the cosmic male and female forces within the psyche. Intoxication is partaking of the bliss of pure consciousness. This inner formulation of the left-handed path is in harmony with the right-handed path. It is only the literal formulation of the left-handed path, not the left-handed path itself which differs from traditional Yoga.

All religions contain symbolic approaches, and they are common in yogic traditions. When the Vedic God Indra is lauded as eating three hundred buffaloes and drinking three lakes of wine, or when he is said to kill his own father, this is a dramatic symbolism. The meat and wine refer to the conquering of the senses. The father to be killed is the ego. When Buddhists are asked to kill the Buddha, it is a symbolic gesture, obviously not to be taken literally, meaning that we should break our attachment to the outer form of the teacher. In fact much of the strange symbolism found in Tantric texts — like sexual union with one's mother — could hardly be taken literally! The mother symbolizes the Kundalini, in which one is to merge.

The yogic tradition as a whole has never been attached to mere words or names and forms. The use of strange or symbolic utterances is common in yogic teachings to provoke deeper inquiry within the mind. To take these things literally is to miss their point altogether.

The Literal Tradition

Left-handed Tantra includes a tradition of using the five forbidden things as part of sacred rituals. The use of the five forbidden things may be recommended as a preliminary practice for individuals who are looking to transcend body-consciousness as the ultimate goal, but who are seeking to do it by degrees. As going beyond the senses is a difficult goal for anyone to achieve, certain intermediate steps can aid in the process. This is the main reason that such practices are done in traditional Tantra.

It is hard to give up our attachments directly, particularly when we come from a materialistic culture. Attachments are the products of many births and are genetically ingrained within us, as well as being constantly reinforced by the environment. There is also an organic process of growth for the soul. We may have to experience certain things before we are capable of going beyond them. One of the ways to transcend a desire is to turn it into a sacred action and offer it up to the Deity.

Some Tantric teachers consider that forbidden actions or substances, like the five forbidden things, have their place when used occasionally in order to break through attachments, particularly the attachment to purity. In the yogic tradition there are three gunas or qualities that bind the soul. Attachment to Tamas, which is darkness and dullness, includes attachment to sex or intoxicants. Attachment to Rajas, which is activity and turbulence, includes attachment to willful spiritual practices or to self-expression like art and music. Attachment to Sattva, which is purity, consists in attachment to the idea of being holy and to a life-style of purity.

Those attached to Sattva are not really free, but caught up in the appearance of being spiritual people. The idea of purity becomes a subtle obstacle to their further spiritual growth. There are instances when Tantric teachers encourage such disciples to do something forbidden — something Rajasic or Tamasic — in order to break the disciple's attachment to Sattva. This may not consist merely of the five forbidden things. It may consist of drinking unclean water, meditating in a cremation ground, or otherwise breaking the rules of purity, caste and custom.

This method is most appropriate for those individuals attached to Sattva (purity), like traditional Hindus or Buddhists with their rules, restrictions and conservative social customs. In modern Western culture we are attached to Rajas and Tamas (drama and sensation). In our case, Tantric methods to break attachment to Sattva are seldom needed because it is not Sattva that we are attached to! Such methods appeal to our basic urge to indulge further in Rajas and Tamas or drama and sensation, and will cause our attachments to increase. Thus the application of this method does not seem appropriate in our circumstance, though it may have its validity in other settings. Those who use the methods of left-handed Tantra as such occasional shock treatment generally follow right-handed Tantra and are not in favor of any widespread use of these methods.

Forbidden Practices as the Direct Path

This brings us to the tradition which uses the practices of left-handed Tantra as a means of direct realization. We may observe that this group is a minority even among the followers of left-handed Tantra.

Such Tantrics holds that ordinary human indulgences can be regularly applied, at least for a certain period, as a means of spiritual realization. Yet even among them there is variation in their views. Some allow sexual union, for example, but do not prescribe taking meat, which involves violence to animals. As the principle of ahimsa (non-violence) is strong in all yogic traditions, actions involving violence to any creatures are seldom approved of. Such Tantric masters claim that by taking our indulgences to an extreme we can see their limitations and go beyond them. Or they may claim to be able to harness the energies of negative emotions, like wrath or lust, to transform us on a deep level of the mind.

Some Tantric masters may claim that they have transcended all rules and are able to do whatever they wish — that sensual indulgences cannot bind them. Some of these teachers may have their disciples follow strict codes of purity even when they themselves do not. Others may allow their disciples to indulge, even in extreme ways, under their guidance. Such teachers, acting in an unorthodox or unspiritual manner, may claim to be breaking our attachment to mere appearances and preconceptions about spiritual teachers that blind us to the real truth inside ourselves.

I do not want to state that such a path is not possible. However, I would emphasize that it is a rare and dangerous approach which deprives us of the safeguards designed to protect us along the spiritual path. Moreover, this approach definitely caters to human weaknesses and can easily be exploited. It can be used to justify ordinary human indulgences, or to encourage indulging in them on an abnormal scale. It appeals to the excesses of our age: sex, violence and entertainment. Even those who teach this approach usually consider it to be a dangerous path, not suitable for many people, though many may find the idea of it appealing (which is generally a sign that such a path is *not* suitable). It is wrong to think that such a path is characteristic of Tantra or that true Tantra requires it.

THE THIRD OR DIRECT PATH

A third Tantric path exists, which is the Tantric version of the direct path. Sometimes, the third path is regarded as the higher part of the right-handed approach (or even the left-handed approach). On this path the yogi gives up outer ritualistic forms of worship, recognizing their flaws. Any outward, formal, or substance-oriented action can keep the mind bound to the external world. While such actions purify our minds, to take them as our primary practice cannot take us far along the path of realization.

The yogi also gives up internal forms of worship like the chanting of mantras which constitute the right-handed path. These too have their rules and regulations which are cumbersome and can attach the mind to mental activity. The highest yogi merely inquires into his own nature and becomes one with the True Self — which is the real meaning of searching out the lotus feet of the Mother. This highest Tantric path is the path of Self-inquiry, or Atma-vichara, which is also the highest Vedantic path. It consists of tracing the I-thought back to its origin in pure awareness. All of our thoughts originate from the I-thought. However, this I in its true nature is unknown to us because we are always associating it with some transient quality or object like the body, or whatever we are identified with in the form of "I am this" or "This is mine." Discarding the object portion from the I-thought, we can discover our true nature which transcends all objectivity and the limitations of time and space that objectivity requires.

Yet as this is the highest path, few are really able to tread it, and most who approach it do not go beyond the mere concept of it. We can easily speculate about the Higher Self, but it is quite another thing to actually still the mind. Such speculative thought can be a trap. It is no substitute for real practice, and is inferior to the practice of mantra in its ability to calm the mind. In fact, some yogis think that unless one is proficient in the practice of mantra, one will not have the proper concentration for true Self-inquiry.

The lesser paths, though they have their limitations, are often more realistic to tread. Usually we need to do some daily preliminary rituals. We also may need to do mantras to develop the power of attention, which may take years to perfect, before direct meditation approaches are viable. Even if it is possible for us to engage in direct meditation, mantra remains helpful as a support practice. Mantra develops the mental force to allow us to proceed with meditation. While recognizing the value of the highest teachings, we should understand how to approach them. Even those who can practice deep meditation spontaneously may find that their practice is stronger if rituals and mantras are included in their daily regimen.

The Tantric approach is very practical. We should do the highest practice that we are really capable of, but not overlook anything that might be helpful, however apparently insignificant. We should not attach ourselves to inferior practices, but we should do what is possible for us, even if it is a very simple ritual or just being careful with our diet. The form is not what matters but increasing the energy of our consciousness in our daily lives. The methods of Tantra, though form-oriented or ritualistic, have the same goal of Self-realization as direct meditation approaches, and serve to lead us to these higher practices.

3
LEVELS OF
TANTRIC TEACHING

*I don't know your mantra or your yantra. How can I
know how to praise you? I don't know how to call you or
how to meditate upon you, how can I know how to praise
you?*

*I don't know your mudra, Mother I only know that
taking refuge in you is the means of alleviating all afflic-
tion.*

*By ignorance of your law, by having no wealth, by
laziness, by not having the power to act, I have fallen at
your feet.*

*Forgive me, auspicious Mother who carry all the
worlds. A bad son is born sometimes but there is never a
bad mother. — Shankaracharya, Prayer to the Goddess
for Forgiveness of Sins 1–2*

In this chapter we will outline the different levels and aspects of
Tantric teachings. This is to prepare the foundation for our examination
of the worship of the Goddess and the practice of Tantric Yoga in the
following sections of the book. As we explore the different forms of the
Goddess, we will note the many different levels of significance each
Goddess relates to and the many different ways in which her energy can
be contacted. We may not easily associate all these approaches with an
idea of a Goddess or even of worship. Many of these approaches are
philosophical, abstract, or formless and far removed from any image of
the feminine. According to the Hindu idea the Goddess manifests on all
levels of the universe from the physical to Pure Consciousness and is not
limited to the idea or form of the human female.

To the Hindu devotee of the Goddess there is no contradiction between
the Goddess represented in a particular anthropomorphic form and the
Goddess appearing as the Absolute beyond all creation. Seeing the
Goddess in a particular form not only allows us to approach her on the
most common level of sense perception, it allows her transcendent reality

to be perceived in manifestation. The Vedic view that the "Brahman is all" requires seeing the Divine in every form as well as beyond all form.

The Hindu mind, like that of many traditional peoples, is able to personify what are to us mere abstract or spiritual truths, and worship them in the forms of various Gods and Goddesses. What we might philosophically think of as the eternal, the Hindu mind will worship as the Goddess Kali, for example. Spiritual ideas are clothed in a concrete imagery and approached as a living being. This does not reflect a lack of development of the intellect or an attachment to form. On the contrary, it demonstrates an experiential contact with higher truths as living realities. Thus the various approaches of Tantric worship combine the highest philosophy with the most concrete experience and vivid imagination, not out of a kind of contradiction, but through a comprehensive understanding and synthetic perception.

Tantra aims at a personal relationship between ourselves and cosmic reality, which is to directly experience truth in our daily lives. Tantra teaches that consciousness is the sole reality in the universe. Hence all things can be approached and communed with as if they were conscious, because in truth they are. As part of consciousness each thing in the universe, including ideas, can be communed with and spoken to as if to another person. Thus we should address all aspects of life — including not only plants and animals but inanimate nature and even our own emotions — as forms of the Gods and Goddesses or as Divine powers and presences. Ultimately we must discover that all aspects of the universe are parts of our own nature — which is not merely human, but the nature of transcendent Awareness.

Tantra is concerned with providing us tools to discover truth for ourselves rather than promoting any particular dogma or ideology. Tantric tools consist of the whole range of spiritual practices, from ritual to formless meditation approaches. Tantric texts prescribe the worship of the Goddess. However, the term worship is not entirely appropriate. From a Judeo-Christian perspective worship primarily means propitiation of the Divine outside of ourselves through prayer and ritual. In the Hindu sense, worship is a means of uniting with the deity as one's own inmost nature. Worship implies the practice of Yoga and has many levels of approach, of which prayer is only one. Its main method is meditation.

THE MEANING OF SHAKTI

The Goddess or cosmic feminine force in Tantra is worshipped as Shakti, generally translated as "power," whereas the God or cosmic masculine force is worshipped as Shiva, meaning "peace." Yet to render

Shakti as power creates many misconceptions. Shakti is the power of Shiva or the power of peace. It is not power born of violence or aggression. It is the power born in passivity, in silence of mind, the energy which comes forth from the Void, like the life that comes forth from the womb. Shakti is not a power which is asserted against something, but a power that enlivens everything from within.

In the Shiva-Shakti concept the male is passive and the female is active, whereas in Buddhist thought the male (upaya or skill) is active and the female is passive (prajña or wisdom). Similarly, in the Vaishnava tradition Vishnu or Krishna (consciousness or love), the male force, is active, whereas Lakshmi or Radha (beauty or devotion), the female force, is passive. However, Shakti is the power of wisdom and devotion. Shiva is the passivity of the will, which accomplishes all things without itself moving. Whether the male or female are active or passive is thus a matter of different roles and levels, not of any fundamental difference between these formulations.

In addition, Shakti is not an external power but Svashakti, one's own power. To worship the Shakti is to take back one's own power, which is to recognize the power of one's own consciousness, the womb in which the energy of enlightenment is born.

Shakti is the descent of Divine grace, which is the power of peace. Woman has the power and potency to create new life. She has the energy of beauty, delight and creativity. This transformative power of the Divine Mother is the Shakti that works behind all great changes in the universe, and brings the human being to the greatest transformation, which is enlightenment. The purpose of Tantra is to energize that Shakti dormant within us by unfolding all the different levels and rhythms of her movement, as she naturally seeks her native abode in the Supreme.

TANTRA, MANTRA AND YANTRA

There are three main aspects of Tantric teachings — Tantra, Mantra and Yantra — which usually go together. The Tantra is the teaching, which represents the reality we are seeking to realize. The Mantra is the sound-form of the deity, which is the power of consciousness that is the main propulsion toward realization. The Yantra is a geometrical design on which various mantras may be inscribed, through which the deity, the Tantra and the Mantra can be visualized and internalized.

However, it is possible to chant the Mantra of a Deity without studying its corresponding Tantra or teaching. One can use a Yantra — as in the widespread use of the Sri Yantra as a meditation or design symbol

— without knowing its Tantra or Mantra, though such practice is not considered complete.

Mantra

Each deity has a specific mantra, which is its mental form. Deities have single seed-syllable or bija mantras, like Om for Tara or Hrīm for Bhuvaneshvari, and an extended mantra, which may contain the name of the deity along with various other words. For each mantra there is a seer, which in the case of the Goddess is her corresponding consort or form of Lord Shiva.

Each deity also has various Vedic and Puranic verses or mantras that can be used in its worship. Stotras or hymns of praise to the deities, as found in various Tantric and Puranic works, can be used in their worship. Stotras to the Goddess by the great Vedantic teacher Shankaracharya are among the best, particularly *Saundarya Lahiri*, the Wave of Bliss.

YANTRA AND MANDALA

The most significant Yantra is the Sri Yantra, but there are separate Yantras for each of the Ten Wisdom Forms of the Goddess, and for most Hindu Gods and Goddesses. Yantras represent a more subtle level of reality than the anthropomorphic image of the deity. They show the energy or law body of the deity. Mandalas are extended Yantras which contain meditation forms of deities as well as various mantras and other designs. Yantras should be inscribed in metal, like copper, silver or gold, as metal is best able to hold the power of the Yantra. However, Yantras inscribed on silk or wool are also useful (but not on cotton). Yantras may be meditated upon according to specific colors. In fact some yantras for different deities — like those for Dhumavati, Matangi and Kamala among the Ten Wisdom Goddesses — are the same except for differences in color. For those wishing to use yantras there are various sources now which sell them along with other tools for Tantra and devotional worship, like statues of Gods and Goddesses.

The Six-Pointed Star

The God and Goddess or Shiva and Shakti have certain prime forms. Generally Shiva is the ascending force, Shakti is the descending force. In this regard Shiva is the upward pointed triangle and Shakti the downward pointed triangle. The six-pointed star is thus one of the most important Tantric symbols and the basis of most Yantras. Even the Sri Yantra combines various downward pointed and upward pointing triangles, usually five pointed downward and four pointing up.

SRI CHAKRA/SRI YANTRA

Sri Chakra/Sri Yantra

Sri Chakra also known as Sri Yantra is the most important of the Yantras. The most famous form of the Sri Chakra is its a three dimensional form, which is sometimes made in metal. In this way Sri Chakra is said to represent Mount Meru, the cosmic mountain at the center of the universe. Sri Chakra is the main Yantra of the Goddess and all aspects of her worship can be performed through it. It can also be used to worship Shiva.

MEDITATION FORMS

Typical Tantric teachings present a form (murti) of the deity to visualize and meditate upon. Each deity has a subtle body form for meditation or contemplation (Dhyana Murti). The deity appears in a certain color, making certain gestures, carrying certain weapons, wearing certain ornaments, and so on. These are revealed in various meditation verses on the deity (Dhyana Shloka). The meditation form is the initial way to contact the deity and to energize its power within our psyche, as we most respond to human forms in our daily life. We should seek to commune with the form of the deity. If we meditate upon it strongly enough the form will come alive and teach us, and reveal the deeper aspects of its reality.

WORSHIP AND YOGA

Worship of the deity is twofold, outer and inner. Outer worship consists of making various offerings like flowers or incense to the form of the deity or its yantra. Inner worship requires meditation. Inner worship can involve doing an imaginary form of outer worship, like offering imaginary gems or flowers to the deities, or other Yoga practices like repeating the mantra of the deity along with certain breathing practices (pranayama). However, outer worship is also done along with the use of mantra and meditation and may be done as preliminary to inner worship. Hence Tantric worship is primarily meditation. It does not mean worshipping a deity outside of oneself, but bringing the powers of our own Divine Self-nature into manifestation. Tantric worship is the practice of Yoga.

EXTERNAL METHODS: RITUAL

Puja

The standard form of Hindu worship, whether Tantric or Puranic, is puja. The most typical form of Hindu puja is Ganesh puja, as Ganesh, the elephant-faced God, removes obstacles to allow for all forms of worship to be successful. There are special pujas to the different forms of the Goddess as well.

Simple puja involves the offering of five things to the deity. These are a fragrant oil (for the earth element); a flower (for ether); incense (for air); a flame, as from a ghee lamp (for fire); and liquid food (for water). The statue of the deity can be bathed in various substances like water, milk, yogurt, ghee, or sugar cane juice. It may be garlanded with flowers or adorned with clothes.

If one has a statue or picture of a deity in the house, one should at least offer incense to it or burn a flame before it on a regular basis. This creates a favorable psychic field or sacred space for meditation. It is best to burn a nutritive oil like ghee or sesame for the lights used on puja altars, not wax candles, as the food quality of the oil aids in nourishing the subtle form of the deity. Offering fruit or liquid food like milk or rice gruel is also helpful for the same reason. The subtle or astral forms of the deity must be fed to sustain its contact with the physical world.

Puja involves Prana-pratishta, putting life (Prana) into the icon. Without energizing the icon with an energy of life, love, and consciousness it is no more than an inert object. Puja is a science of energizing material objects with subtle energies, to connect physical reality with a deeper reality. It is not a worship of mere things as Divine.

Homa

The standard form of Vedic worship, which also has both outer and inner applications, is called homa or fire offering. Such fire offerings are incorporated into Tantric rituals, and there is a Buddhist system of Homa as well. Homa is more formal than a puja, and generally has more power to neutralize negative forces as well as to increase those which are positive. It also requires more work to do and takes more preparation. Hence it is more typically done on special occasions. However a simple homa, called Agnihotra or the fire-offering, is done daily at the rising and setting of the sun and at noon.

Fuel for homa includes cow dung, special types of wood, and offerings of items like rice grains, ghee (clarified butter), and sweet cakes. The fire takes the subtle essence of the offerings and conveys them to the deity. Along with the offering, the fire conducts our thoughts and wishes. If we offer positive thoughts into the fire, like the wish for universal peace, it strengthens and magnifies them. If we offer negative thoughts, like fear or anger, it helps burn them up.

INTERNAL METHODS: YOGA PRACTICES

Yogic worship consists of internal rituals involving speech, breath and mind. Puja can be done with the mind (Manasa Puja), a process which consists of imagining the deity and the different offerings given to it. There are certain hymns or Stotras that describe mental puja, and which can be very elaborate since the items involved are only imaginary. The deity can be worshipped in the different chakras of the subtle body by concentrating on its Mantra, Yantra or Murti in these locations.

Pranayama (breathing practices) can be done to the deity, using its mantra, or directing the breath to the center (chakra) the deity is imagined as residing. Pranayama and mantra go together. Mantra serves to internalize pranayama, which in turn empowers the mantra. The chanting of mantras can be done silently or in a low voice. Generally the mental repetition of the mantra is best as it serves to better internalize the mind. Mantras can be combined with the breath, using certain mantras for inhalation, retention and exhalation. Mantras are the simplest and perhaps most effect method of Tantric practice. There is no Tantra without Mantra.

DIRECT METHODS: MEDITATION
Pure Worship (Shuddha Upasana)

The pure worship of the deity consists of various meditative methods to understand its inner reality. Such practices usually have nothing to do with any forms. They may not even use mantra and yantra. For example, meditation on the source of the breath is the pure worship or Shuddha Upasana for the Goddess Kali, who symbolizes the Prana or life-force. The meditative worship of the deities involves various modes of inquiry, awareness practices, or contemplations of certain truths.

Shiva Linga

The Linga and Yoni

Tantric forms derive from the basic forces and forms of nature and its underlying cosmic intelligence. They are representations of cosmic energy in its various laws and unfoldment. Shiva, the cosmic masculine force, as an ascending energy is represented as a pillar, column, standing stone, pyramid, or obelisk. Shakti, the cosmic feminine force, is a ring or circle in which the central standing stone is placed. The combination of a standing stone surrounded by a ring is the basis of the Shiva linga, a pillar-like standing stone (linga) placed in ring or dish (yoni). Containing the two basic symbols of Shiva and Shakti, it is the prime symbol both of Shaivism and Tantra.

The worship of Shiva and Shakti is closely associated with the mountains and with the yogis who retire to mountain regions to pursue their practices. Shakti is born from the mountain (Parvata) and hence she is called Parvati. Yet Shiva himself is a mountain, particularly in the form of massive stony mountains that jut in triangular forms above treeline, which are common in the high Himalayas. Above treeline a spiritual energy is accessible to the mind which cannot be found at lower elevations. The massive stony mountains of South India also often look like Shiva lingas. Shiva is the mountain down which the river of heaven, the heavenly Ganges, flows to the Earth. In Hindu mythology the Ganges descends from the head of Shiva. The Shiva linga is also the mountain of the spine, from which the heavenly river or Sushumna flows.

Shakti is a mountain stream or waterfall. She is also a mountain lake, cave, chasm, valley, marsh or meadow. She is round mountains or stones as well as fissures in the mountain rocks. Wherever there are the ascending forms of Shiva there must be the descending forms of Shakti, just as high mountains must create deep valleys and cascading streams. The mountain is a universal symbol of meditation, whereas the mountain stream symbolizes the flow of grace that descends through meditation. The mountain lake is a symbol of the delight of meditation. There are a number of natural Shiva lingas in mountain regions where it is common to find round lakes placed immediately below high mountains much like the shape of the Shiva linga. The Shiva linga, like the Sri Chakra, is a symbol of the cosmic mountain. The three dimensional form of the Sri Chakra is also a Shiva linga.

Most ancient cultures have their standing stones, megaliths, pyramids and obelisks as part of the universal religion of nature and light that we find throughout ancient cultures. The *Vedas* speak of the worship of the pillar (stambha, skambha, daruna, dharma), which is the origin of the Shiva linga. The Shiva linga is sometimes seen as a mortar and pestle used for extracting the Soma, with the mortar being the yoni and the pestle being the linga. The linga is the central ray of solar energy of which the yoni is the peripheral circle.

The Shiva linga is a yin-yang symbol, a representation of the two great cosmic powers, the masculine and the feminine in their eternal embrace. While it does resemble the human genitals in an embrace, Shiva linga worship is not merely worship of the human genitals, as some have suggested. The symbol is not a representation of sex; rather the sexual organs are one of the manifestations of the cosmic forces represented by the symbol.

The Shiva linga symbolizes the power of the awakened crown chakra, the power of spiritual knowledge. It is ritually bathed in water and oil, showing the nectar and wisdom that comes forth from fully energized awareness. In the Bible there is a story of the Patriarch Jacob who, while sleeping on a stone, had a dream of climbing a ladder to heaven. He took the stone and bathed it in oil as in the Hindu practice, and set it forth as a sacred site. This shows that the worship of the Shiva linga was found in the Near East in Biblical times.

The purpose of the Shiva linga therefore is not a glorification of ordinary sexuality, any more than are the Tantric images of the Gods and Goddesses in a sexual embrace. Rather, the linga is an attempt to portray the higher unity of the cosmic masculine and feminine forces, which is what we are really seeking through sexuality. Worshipping the two powers helps us transmute ordinary sexual desire. Hence these symbols are used as a means of redirecting sexual energy, not as a means of ordinary indulgence. The Shiva linga shows the eternal embrace of the Divine masculine and feminine powers which is all that we are truly seeking in life. In this regard Shiva lingas are found in most of the temples and monasteries of India. Many temples have as their central icon not any representational form but a rock in the form of linga or yoni. Many of the oldest icons in India are such rocks.

The forms of Shiva and Devi personify these great forces of nature such as are embodied in the rocks. These same forces appear in the stars and on all levels where energy is manifesting itself. We should view the forms of the Goddess and the ways of worshipping her as means of contacting the great forces of Nature and the universe.

✳ ✳ ✳

Four are the levels of speech. Those of spiritual wisdom know them all. Three placed in secrecy cannot be manipulated. Mortals speak only with the fourth.
— *Rig Veda I.164.45*

The essence of Tantra is Mantra Yoga, which is not only the repetition of sacred sounds but encompasses all means of energizing the mind. According to Tantra the mind consists primarily of sound. Working with sound, whether as mantra, music or vibration is central to energization of the mind.

According to Vedic and Tantric thought the Goddess is the Divine Word, which has a feminine nature. According to the *Vedas*, in the beginning was the Word and the Word was the Goddess. Speech has several levels of manifestation, which are keys to the nature and function of the Goddess. Tantra, like the *Vedas*, recognizes four levels of speech.

Name	Speech	Location	State
VAIKHARI	Audible Speech	Throat	Waking State
MADHYAMA	Thought	Heart	Dream State
PASHYANTI	Illumined Speech	Navel	Deep Sleep
PARA	The Transcendent	Root Center	Samadhi

Vaikhari refers to the coarse or literal level of speech. Most of the time our minds stay on this level of audible speech and conventional meanings of words, which is the level of speech that relates to sensation. We only enter into Madhyama, which literally means the "middle level," when we think deeply about something, when we ponder or wonder about things. Most artistic thinking comes from this level, which reveals the beauty of form and has a creative force. The third level, Pashyanti or the illumined Word, occurs when we perceive the underlying cosmic truth or archetype behind the object or event. Its nature is light or revelation and it reveals the seed forces at work in the universe. We only reach this level through deep meditation or as an act of grace. The fourth level, Para, is the level of pure silence wherein meaning is so full and complete that it cannot be broken down into words. This is the level of pure consciousness, the Divine Word of silence: "I am All."

The power of speech must be brought down to the base of the spine (root chakra) to allow the energy of consciousness to ascend upward as Kundalini to awaken our higher potentials. Before our consciousness ascends, our energy must first descend and penetrate to the depths of our being. To bring the power of speech inward and down is the work of Mantra Yoga and also that of Vedic music (Gandharva Veda) or any spiritual music. To bring speech downward, the breath along with the sound-current of the mind must be brought down to the corresponding centers of the subtle body. In Vaikhari the breath and sound-current is centered in the throat. In Madhyama it is centered at the heart. In Pashyanti its power is in the navel. In Para it merges into the Sushumna at the root chakra.

There are three additional levels of speech, which correspond to the first three levels integrated into the fourth, making seven in all. They are called by their combined names, Para-Pashyanti, Para-Madhyama, and Para-Vaikhari. Para-Pashyanti is the level in which transcendent speech or silence of mind becomes expressed in illumined perception. Para-Madhyama is when it is expressed in profound thought. Para-Vaikhari is when it is expressed in audible speech. This is the highest level of speech which occurs when the human being utters the Divine Word in human language. This is the utterance of the seer or Rishi, from which level the *Vedas* were spoken.

The middle level, Madhyama, is important as the central level, through which all the other levels can be integrated. The middle level of speech in harmony with the Supreme (Para-Madhyama) allows the full integration of knowledge and delight in the spiritual heart. The illumined level of speech allied with the supreme (Para-Pashyanti) allows for the maximum development of wisdom. Tantric Goddesses correspond to these different levels and functions of the Divine Word and are used to energize them, as we will discover in the next section of the book.

PART II

THE TANTRIC TEACHING

Only if Shiva is united with Shakti does he have the power to act, otherwise the God is not even able to quiver.

Thus having been lauded by the creator, preserver and destroyer of the world, how can a man without virtue like myself be able to sing or to praise you?
— *Shankaracharya, Saundarya Lahari 1*

The knowers of the Vedas call you the Goddess of Speech, the housewife of the creator of the universe, the lotus consort of the preserver, the companion of the destroyer, the daughter of the mountain.

Yet as the fourth and transcendent, whose supreme greatness is difficult to approach, Goddess of great magic wisdom, you make the entire universe revolve, as the power of the Supreme Reality.
— *Shankaracharya, Saundarya Lahari 98*

THE TEN WISDOM FORMS OF THE GODDESS
AN INTRODUCTION

THE GODDESS AS KNOWLEDGE

In Tantra, as in many spiritual traditions, the feminine aspect of Divine reality represents knowledge or wisdom (Sanskrit vidya). The three *Vedas*, the most ancient scriptures of the Hindu tradition — which represent the three faculties of speech, mind and breath — are called the Trayi Vidya or the three wisdoms (feminine). The Greek idea of three Graces is similar.

The true worship of the Goddess involves knowledge, which is her real form. It is not merely an outer worship, but an inner worship which is meditation. Meditation on the Goddess is a form of Self-inquiry or a means of acquiring knowledge. It is not merely an adulation of feminine forms or qualities. It may start with the image of the Goddess but reaches far beyond the limits of name, form and personality to the impersonal Absolute.

The Goddess represents what is hidden, secret, subtle and sensitive, what has to be searched out and discovered. As the Word, she represents both the teaching and its comprehension. She is thus the inner guiding power. The Goddess represents what is to be known, what we are drawn by an inner fascination to discover. She is the mystery and allure of the higher knowledge which causes us to lose interest in what the mind can know, the familiar realm of the senses. The Goddess takes us beyond the realm of the known and the domain of time-space into the secrets of eternity-infinity.

In the process of spiritual learning the Goddess becomes the muse who guides and inspires us. She is the high priestess who unfolds the inner truths. Yet true knowledge as part of an integral comprehension of reality is always related to energy and beauty. The Goddess is not only knowledge but power and delight. Knowledge of her reveals her powers, which are awesome and transformative. Understanding of her reveals her bliss, which is the joy of going beyond all the limitations of the body-mind.

Yet the Goddess does not merely give us knowledge. She is the knowledge. The inner knowledge is the body of the Goddess, which she unfolds as her various adornments and eventually as her own being. Wisdom is the ultimate form of beauty and delight, the most sought after beloved object in creation, and hence the ultimate embodiment of the Divine feminine.

Spiritual knowledge is the womb through which we are reborn into the world of truth. Knowledge is the Divine Mother through whom we are born as Gods. Entering into the higher knowledge is to enter into the body of the Goddess for our own spiritual rebirth. To contact the Divine Mother and commune with her powers unfolds the various degrees and stages of our own inner transformation.

Ultimately the Goddess is not merely knowledge but pure consciousness itself (Samvit). She bestows the capacity to cognize the underlying unitary essence in all beings. She is the knowledge that puts the mind to rest and returns us to the source. Through her we discover the serenity of the Self.

THE TEN WISDOM FORMS OF THE GODDESS

Hindu deities represent the Divine consciousness functioning on all levels of the universe, both outwardly and inwardly. They have a broad range of meaning — form and formless, concrete and abstract, human and non-human, terrible and beautiful. They appear on every level of our being and of the world being, as the various principles, energies and faculties which make up this great universe, manifest and unmanifest. The Goddess, who represents creation on all levels, possess this same diversity, which is expressed through her Ten Wisdom Forms (Dasha Mahavidya) and their different functions.

Dasha Mahavidya means the "Ten Great Knowledges." They reveal the inner workings of both the universe and the psyche, once the veil of appearances is pulled down. They represent the deeper truths of life hidden behind our attachment to the outer forms of things. Their messages are sometimes inspiring and sometimes frightening because they represent life itself, but they are always instructive to those who are looking for something beyond the ordinary realm.

The Ten Forms of the Goddess function not merely to teach us superficially or intellectually but to challenge us to look deeper. As great cosmic forces their energies can be difficult to bear and their extremes of appearance and expression may jolt us. Their forms are often disturbing, and they are not meant to be merely pleasant. They are meant, like mysteries, to entrance or shock the mind into awakening. They are not meant to merely console or inspire but to promote within us the deepest search. Their forms are ambiguous, contradictory and paradoxical. They are provocative energies designed to take hold of our minds and through their enigmatic nature neutralize the thought process which keeps us in bondage.

Life itself is something awesome and mysterious. We do not know why we are born or when we will die. We do not even know how we move, breathe or think. Most of what we are seeking and struggling for in life is merely transient and does not answer the ultimate question of our destiny: what, if anything, in us transcends death. Our knowledge only grasps the surface of the world, and we do not have any real sense of our ultimate identity. To approach the higher knowledge we must set the lower knowledge aside, which is not to reject it altogether but to recognize its limited place. The Wisdom Forms of the Goddess are part a spiritual science, which we can examine only when we have set aside our outer knowing and its grasping for information and ideas.

Yet this spiritual science is also an art. It cannot be approached mechanically but requires creative participation. We must become that reality and experience within ourselves all of its manifold dimensions. We must become the Goddess as her power comes to work through us. This way of yogic knowledge is a theater or play in the mind. It contains all of life and all of the universe as flowing through our own nervous system. It is perhaps the ultimate of all experiences, as through it experience itself is dissolved into the transcendent.

Each of the Ten Forms of the Goddess represents a particular approach to Self-realization, to knowledge of that within us which transcends time and transient identity. Yet each of the ten has within itself many layers. Unless we are willing to look deeply, we may become caught in a secondary aspect of the form or function of the Goddess. As the representatives of powerful cosmic forces, the Goddesses can be approached to gain health, wealth, fame or other ordinary goals of life. However, if we approach them with a selfish intention, their inner powers cannot come forth. We cannot manipulate these deep cosmic forces, we can only benefit from them if we honor the wisdom at their origin. Hence these Knowledge Forms should not to be approached superficially or casually. For them to really work, we must first surrender to the Divine Mother herself and gain her grace. It is her power, her Yoga Shakti that does the work. We can be receptive to its current and learn its rhythms, but we cannot direct its flow. We must not try to use these teachings out of personal willfulness, or they will not be liberating for us.

The Ten Forms of the Goddess make up a complete and integral teaching but several of them have their own special worship as representing the Supreme Mother herself. Sundari, also called Lalita or Rajarajeshvari, is the most popular form of the Divine Mother in South India (which tradition the author of this book follows). In the north and west of India, in Tibet and Kashmir and in Buddhist lands, Tara has this importance. In the north and east of India, Bengal and Assam, which is the region of India where the worship of the Goddess has always been the most popular, Kali represents the Great World Mother. Kali is the first and foremost of the Ten Wisdom Goddesses. All ten can be portrayed as various aspects of Kali. They are often placed around her as their central deity. Hence the Dasha Mahavidya is one of the most important forms of Kali worship.

ORIGIN OF THE TEN WISDOM GODDESSES

The first clear reference to the Ten Wisdom Goddesses occurs in the *Shiva Purana* (V.50). According to this story a demon named Durgama, took control of the four *Vedas*, by a boon of the Creator, Lord Brahma, and through them gained power over the entire universe. This caused a tremendous drought on earth for many years in which all creatures suffered greatly. Hence the Gods called upon the Goddess to save the world. The Goddess, who always responds to the wishes of her devotees, first eliminated the drought and filled all the waters of the earth. Then the Gods asked an additional boon to destroy the great demon and reclaim the *Vedas*. In her battle with the demon, the Goddess brought ten great forms out of her body — the Dasha Mahavidya — and then took the forms of innumerable Goddesses. She defeated the demon and returned the *Vedas* to the Gods. As the conqueror of Durgama, the Goddess was named Durga.

The Ten Wisdom Goddesses are originally associated with the myth of restoring the Vedic teaching, which through the process of time had fallen under the forces of decay and corruption. From the *Vedas* to the *Tantras* is an unbroken line of mantric and meditation teachings centered in the Goddess, who herself is the Divine Word and the *Vedas*, and who periodically renovates the teaching in order to sustain it in this world bound by time and death.

KALI YANTRA

1
KALI
The Goddess of Yogic Transformation

Om: Victorious, auspicious Kali, beneficent Kali, who carries the skull, the deliverer, forgiveness, peace, the supporter of all, the Divine offering, the ancestral offering, reverence to You!

Be victorious, Goddess who destroys all passions! Be victorious, you who remove the afflictions of all beings! Be victorious, Goddess who pervades all. As the dark night of time, reverence to You!

— vi Mahatmya, Argala Stotra 1–2, Markendeya Purana

Kali is perhaps the most mysterious and difficult to understand of the Goddesses of India. She is dark, destructive, terrible in form, and unpredictable. She is allied with the forces of death and appears alien to any of our ordinary esthetic preferences. She is not a beautiful madonna, nor enticing Goddess, but an enigma, a threat, perhaps even a curse. Yet for this same reason Kali has a fascination which more consoling and pleasing forms cannot have. It is not enough merely to adore the sublime; we must first cross over the terrible. This is the allure of Kali.

As the chosen Deity worshipped by Paramahansa Ramakrishna, one of the most well known modern teachers within the Hindu tradition, Kali is one of the most commonly known of Hindu Goddesses, but still not well understood. Yet much of what we admire in Ramakrishna — his love, bliss, and universal spirit — is Kali's gift to us through him. Through him Kali has already delivered us her message for the modern age.

KALI AND TIME

The Sanskrit word Kali literally means time. Kali is the feminine of the word for time, which in the masculine is Kala. Time, as we all are forced to understand, is the foremost of the powers which governs the universe. In its essential nature time is eternity itself, perpetual changeless duration. Everything changes but change itself. Everything moves but the movement itself does not stop. This perpetuity or immutability in duration is the secret message of time. Ultimately, time is being itself, the unborn,

KALI

uncreate, undying, absolute reality. Time in its manifestation conceals unmanifest time which is eternity, the mirror on which the images of time move but which they cannot affect.

Time is the great force of change that drives all things to grow and develop. Time cooks or ripens all things. Hence this force of time is not a mere process of recurrence. Through repeated births and deaths, through manifold changes, created beings come to realize the ultimate truth of time itself and merge into eternity. Kali is the Goddess who symbolizes this spiral process whereby we grow and evolve into that which goes beyond all form and change.

Why should we look on time as a Goddess or a feminine form? Time is not a mere abstract continuum in which things occur, it is a living field, a conscious energy, a matrix and a vortex. Time is the great womb and hence has a feminine quality.

Time is the working out of a cosmic intelligence. It is the very breath of the cosmic spirit. Time is not a mere mathematical concept but the very stuff of our experience, the rhythm of our lives. What are we apart from time? Time is our mother and origin, as well as our final abode. Time is the mother who eats her own children, which is one of the terrible aspects of Kali. Yet in devouring her own children she is also returning them to her wholeness and delight.

In our own experience, we naturally endow time with feeling because time is inherently feeling or consciousness. We look with nostalgia on the past, even if our past has been difficult. Similarly we look with longing upon the future, however close we are to the end of our lives. Time is birth and death, growth and decay, which is the essence of our existence. Time is our life and hence we look upon it as our own. It *is* our own. And yet we are afraid we will lose it. Kali teaches us that if we give up our attachment to the events of our lives, we gain mastery over time itself. We can devour death and swallow the universe, without moving at all.

We can perceive the feminine nature of time by considering how we relate to it. Time draws us to attach ourselves either to the forms of time or to the being of time which is eternity. The worship of Kali is this merging into eternity, in which the forms of time are negated into the essential being of time as pure existence. Time is either beguiling us to pursue some experience, or educating us to merge into the ground of experience itself which is the eternal presence.

Creation and Destruction

Time is both creation and destruction. To create we must first destroy. To bring the new into being, we must first let go of the old. It is destruction

Goddesses begin with Kali, who is the image of destruction, in which nothing is left, except Lord Shiva himself.

For our spiritual re-creation or resurrection we must first allow the attachment to our material nature to be destroyed. We must go beyond all the bounds of the known and determined, relinquishing all identities, opinions and beliefs. We ourselves must become a sacrificial victim to the Divine. No savior by his sacrifice can save us. Only the sacrifice of our own ego can really deliver us beyond the bonds of ignorance and sorrow. Kali is the form of Divine energy who accepts this offering.

However, not only do we exist in time, we are part of time and partake of its essential nature, which is eternity. Not only do we experience change in our outer nature through the mind-body complex, in our inner nature as pure consciousness we witness change from the standpoint of the timeless. As we grow in consciousness we become time itself and consume the entire universe. This is to become one with Kali, in whom we become able to create and destroy the entire universe at will with our every breath, our every sensation, and our every thought.

Kali as Life and Death

Time is life. Life is our movement in time. Through our own life-force or Prana we experience time. Kali as time is Prana or the life-force. Kali or the Divine Mother is our life. She is the secret power behind the working of our bodily systems and vital energy. Only through her do we live, and it is her intelligence that gives such a marvelous order to the body.

The life-force manifests through the blood. Hence Kali is associated with blood. As the life-force she drinks the blood of all beings. She is life ever renewing itself through our various physiological processes, which are all various sacrificial offerings of matter to the spirit.

Time is our eventual death and the destruction of all things. Hence Kali is also death. Yet death is not merely annihilation but the doorway to the eternal. Death is merely the ending of what has no real substance. It eliminates the inessential to reveal the essential. Spiritual death, the death of the separate self, is the way to eternal life.

Life and death are the rhythms of time, the ebb and flow of the eternal sea. Kali is the life that exists in death and the death that exists in life. To be conscious of life in death and death in life is one of her meditational approaches. To die daily is her daily worship. This is to die to all the things of thought, our worries, cares, anxieties, ambitions, loves and hates, likes and dislikes. It is to daily cast our minds into the highest flame of the fire of awareness. Everyday before we sleep we should empty the mind, as if each day were our last. This also makes each new day our first and turns life itself into a meditation.

Kali is the love that exists at the heart of life, which is the immortal life that endures through both life and death. Maintaining the awareness of the eternal nature of life through the cycles of birth and death is another one of her meditational approaches. The truth is that our soul, our aspiration toward the Divine, which is our eternal love, never has died and never will die. To be conscious of that enduring aspiration is to die to the things of the mind and the senses, and come to know the cosmic life and Divine grace.

Kali is thus death itself in all of its forms and on all levels, but above all, the death of the separate self. Kali is portrayed as dancing in a cremation ground. Meditation on death is another way of contacting the energy of Kali. Death is not only our ultimate end, she is also our origin and mother, as death is our return to eternity.

As a meditative study of Death the Ten Wisdom Forms of the Goddess have much in common with such teachings as the *Egyptian Book of the Dead* and the *Tibetan Book of the Dead*. These teachings are not merely manuals to aid us in our transition when the body dies, they are teachings that show us how to bring about psychological death — the death of separateness — which thereby brings about the resurrection of the Divine Self within us. This is the great action of Kali.

KALI AS BEING

Life or Prana is the manifestation in creation of the eternal principle of Being, Sat. Our desire to live forever reflects our eternal being — the fact that in our true nature we never change, much less pass away. All of us wish, "May I always live."

Kali grants us this eternal life. Yet the eternal life has a price. Only that which is immortal can be immortal, as nothing can change its own nature. The mortal and the transient must pass away. To gain the eternity that is Kali, our mortal nature must be sacrificed. Hence Kali appears frightening and destructive to the ordinary vision.

Yet we all must die. We must lose all of our attachments, including our own body and mind. Our clinging to things has never allowed us to hold on to them anyway. It has only bred frustration because we lose them eventually. Hence the sacrifice of the mortal nature is something that is inevitable. If we do it voluntarily we gain immortality. If we are forced to do it involuntarily, we fall into the confusion of repeated births, in a vain attempt to satisfy our unfulfilled desires.

KALI AS NIRVANA

Kali as the power of death and negation is Nirvana, the state of the dissolution of desire. She functions to extinguish all of our wants and cravings and merge us into the Nirvanic field, the realm of the unborn, uncreate, and unmanifest. Kali develops forms only to take us beyond form. When her force awakens within us she works to break down all limitations and attachments, so that we might transcend the entire field of the known. Kali is Nirvana Shakti or the ultimate power of negation whereby all thoughts are surrendered into the unknowable field of pure being itself. Those who seek to merge themselves into the unknown, formless, uncreate Nirvanic field are true worshippers of Kali.

KALI AS THE ELEMENT OF AIR

On a cosmic level, Kali relates to the element of air or the wind, Vayu. According to Ayurvedic medicine, those of Vata or airy temperament, have a portion of Kali's energy. Like the wind she is mobile, subtle and transformative. Kali relates to lightning (vidyut-shakti) or the electrical force that manifests in the atmosphere. This force pervades the universe as the energy of transformation. It acts quickly, unpredictably, and leaves no trace of itself, yet catalyzes the most radical changes. Kali grants a lightning-like illumination and transformation. She is thus not merely dark. Like the blue-black rain cloud she has her lightning illumination that strikes decisively. She is the lightning perception of truth which negates all illusions and makes the outer world appear dark, and makes us appear dark to the outer world as it takes us from the shadowy realm of visible reality to the invisible supreme light.

In the human body air exists in the form of Prana, the breath or life-force. Kali is our very life-energy, which does not belong to us but to the Divine Mother. This life-energy also brings about our death when it departs from the body on its journey to the subtle worlds. In the movement of the breath we experience the reality of Kali or the great rhythm of life and death.

KALI AS THE POWER OF ACTION

Kali is the power of action or transformation (Kriya-shakti). Through time and breath all things are accomplished. Yet what she accomplishes is not a mere outer action. She accomplishes the spiritual labor of our rebirth into pure consciousness. For this she creates the energy and does the work if we surrender to her force.

If we wish to accomplish any great action, particularly the inner processes of yogic transformation, we should seek the grace of Mother

Kali. Once her force manifests within us, our entire being undergoes a radical change and reorientation that takes us beyond the world.

KALI AS BEAUTY

Kali means beauty. The root kal, from which the name comes, means "to count," "to measure," or "to set in motion," hence "time." It also refers to what is well-formed or measured out, hence beauty. Time itself has a movement, a rhythm, a dance which is the basis of all beauty. This is also the rhythm of the life force which allows for movement.

Yet beauty is not only loveliness, it is also terror or even death. Kali is the beauty that is terror. She is the beautiful woman who so bewitches a man that he loses his head or even his life pursuing her. Kali is thus unattainable beauty or even unrequited love, which shows the Divine mystery that we can never grasp within the realm of form. Actually all beauty is ungraspable because it does not really belong to form but to consciousness itself. The more we seek beauty on the outside, the more we lose our life. The more we seek beauty within, the more we go beyond death. This is also part of the symbolism of Kali.

Divine beauty is terror because it pales all the beauty and glory of mortal life. Beauty is only reflected in form. It really belongs to the eternal. When the flower wilts, as it must, it is not beauty that passes away but merely the form on which beauty is reflected.

KALI AND SHIVA

Kali is the consort of Lord Shiva, who is also Kala or the Lord of Time and eternity. Kali is the active power coming from Lord Shiva, who as transcendent reality is beyond action or motivation. Kali represents the flow of grace from the heart of Shiva. Surrendering to her thus brings us the eternal peace and immortal life of Shiva himself. Shiva is the corpse on whom Kali dances, who is herself the life and energy of Shiva.

Hence we see that Kali is known to all of us in some form or another. She is not the deity of some strange religion but an objective portrayal of essential reality in symbolic form.

LOCATION IN THE BODY

Kali is generally located in the Heart Chakra of the subtle body, the seat of the air element or vayu. Kali relates to the physical heart also, which circulates the life-force, and to the blood itself which carries the life-force. In this form she is called Rakta-Kali or red-Kali. Kali thus is the pulsating of the heart.

In her higher and benefic form as Bhadra (auspicious) Kali she is located in the spiritual heart center, on the right side of the chest. Here she is the giver of the highest transformation, which is Self-realization.

Kali is placed in the middle and is one of the middle or Madhyama forms of speech. She is para-madhyama or the combination of the supreme and middle forms of speech whereby the outer and the inner are mediated together in the heart.

MEDITATION FORM

Kali is dark blue in color and wears a garland of skulls. She has her long tongue sticking out and is laughing. Sometimes instead of a tongue she has two fangs. Kali has four arms and four hands and holds a head chopper with one hand and a severed head dripping blood with the other. With her other two hands she makes the mudras of bestowing boons and dispelling fear. She wears a skirt made of human arms. Kali is portrayed as dancing in a cremation ground and striding on a corpse (who is the form of Lord Shiva himself).

Dark blue is the color of infinite space and eternal time, as well as death. This shows Kali's transcendence of the realm of the known. Her head chopper cuts off the ego. For the ignorant it is the terrible force of death. For the wise it is the power of knowledge, discriminating the eternal from the transient, which gives us the power to break all bondage.

The garland of skulls stands for all the creatures of the world, as well as for our own various incarnations, which are bound to death. The single severed head she carries represents the ego or the I-am-the-body idea that she annihilates. The skulls also show her ability to free our minds from identification with the body. The skirt of arms shows her power over all the organs of action.

The corpse she stands on indicates the inert nature of matter and the body apart from the life-force. The corpse is also Lord Shiva, who indicates the transcendent and inactive nature of pure Being which is the origin of the life-force.

Sometimes Kali is portrayed as an old woman or a hag. Sometimes she is made to look frightening, like a demoness. Other times her face is very beautiful. Sometimes she has the face of a playful young girl. Besides dancing, Kali may be standing or sitting.

MANTRA

Kali's bija mantra or single seed syllable is "krīm," which is the power of action (kriya). The simple repetition of this mantra can be used to worship her. The mantra "klīm" is also used in her worship or just simply the repetition of the name Kali. She also possesses a longer mantra of twenty-two syllables.

Krīm krīm krīm hūm hūm hrīm hrīm dakṣiṇe
kālike krīm krīm krīm hūm hūm hrīm hrīm svāhā!

Hūm is a mantra of wrath and warding off negativity. It also serves to enkindle the fire of spiritual knowledge and Self-inquiry. Hrīm is the mantra of Divine beauty, the descent of grace, purification and transformation. Dakshina is Kali as the power of discernment, which is both right thought and right action. Kalika is another form of the name Kali. Svāhā is the mantra of consecration to the Divine, particularly as the inner or spiritual fire of awareness.

Krīm is repeated three times followed by hūm twice and hrīm twice or a total of seven seed-syllables. Krīm thus emphasizes inner action, which generates the transformative force of hūm, which turns into the ecstatic power of hrīm. These seven syllables can be used by themselves as a mantra to Kali.

The seer of the Kali mantra is Mahakala, Shiva as the great Lord of Time. Only by becoming Time can we gain the power of mind necessary to stand the transforming energy of Kali. Along with the mantra, the Kali Yantra can be used.

Another useful mantra for her is the mantra for Chamunda, the fierce form of Kali, from the story of the *Devi Mahatmya*.

Om aim hrīm klīm cāmuṇḍāyai vicche svāhā!

This mantra consists of the Supreme Word Om followed by the mantras for wisdom, Sarasvati (aim), for purification, Parvati (hrīm), and for transformation, Kali (klīm), and the mantra svāhā, which consummates the offering to Chamunda. Vicche means cut, in the sense of cut off the head of the demon, or cut off the head of the ego.

MEDITATION APPROACHES

There are several meditation approaches for worshipping Kali, apart from those already indicated. As the life-force, Pranayama or breath control is one of the main ways, particularly the silent observance of the breath. This method increases both awareness and longevity. More specifically, Kali relates to the famous So'ham mantra, which is the natural sound of the breath. So relates to inhalation and Ham to exhalation, as the Sanskrit root "Sa" means to take in, to hold, to grasp, or to sit, whereas the root "Ha" means to leave behind, abandon, or destroy. So'ham Pranayama is simple and natural, and yet a direct means of realization.

Ultimately the suspension of the breath in Samadhi is required to understand her reality. This is only possible when we have given up all attachments to the outer world and come to breathe the eternal life-force that comes from consciousness itself.

Since Kali is time or eternity another of her approaches is meditation on the impermanence of all things — an important teaching in Buddhism as well as Hinduism. To see the death or decay inherent in all things is part of her recognition. Those who know the truth of Kali see the old person in the child, and the child in the old man. They see the flower in the decayed stump, and the decayed plant in the flower. They grasp time from both ends and embrace eternity.

RAMAKRISHNA

Paramahansa Ramakrishna, one of the greatest saints of all time, and perhaps the central force behind the modern spiritual awakening of humanity, is the great modern devotee of Kali. He released the tremendous force of Kali-Shakti for the benefit of humanity, setting in motion the forces of transformation to establish a new era for humanity. He is the great modern seer of Kali and perhaps of all the Ten Great Knowledge Forms of the Goddess.

TARA YANTRA

2
TARA
The Saving Word

The ruling lady of speech, like a wish-fulfilling vine around your devotee, you who grant all the accomplishment of all goals, everywhere adorned with all naturally perfect prose and poetry, you who grant realization;
You who are endowed with three eyes like a budding blue lotus, who are an ocean of mercy, shower into our vision your grace with a rain of immortal blessedness.
— *Eight Verses in Praise of Tara, (Tarashtakam) 2*

Tara is not only an important Hindu Goddess, she is also the most important of the Buddhist Goddesses. The Bodhisattva Tara is the consort of the great Buddha Avalokiteshvara, the Lord who looks down with compassion on all living beings. In the Chinese Buddhist tradition she is called Kwan Yin. Among the Ten Wisdom Goddesses Tara resembles Kali and is her first transformation. Time and life (Kali) are related to the sound current or Divine Word, which is Tara. Tara is the power of sound (shabda Shakti), corresponding to Kali as the power of time and transformation. The Word is the consciousness of time, whereas time is the movement of the Word. The Word is the intelligence of time, whereas time is the body of the Word. The creative vibration or the Divine Word is the underlying energy of time.

THE SAVIORESS
The term Tara means the deliverer or savior, from the Sanskrit root tri, meaning "to take across," as to take across a river, the ocean, a mountain, or any difficult situation. The Goddess Tara is called upon in emergencies or at crossroads where we require guidance as to which way to turn. Tara is the saving knowledge. She is the Savioress. The idea of the Goddess as saving wisdom is as old as the *Vedas*, and is a common idea in many spiritual traditions.

Secondly, the term Tara means "a star," as the root tri also means "to scatter" (the stars being scattered in the heavens). Tara is the star of our aspiration, the muse who guides us along the creative path.

TARA

TARA AS OM

The Divine Word in both Hindu and Buddhist systems relates to the mantra Om. Om is the power of sound, called pranava or the original vibration. Tara (masculine, the deliverer) is a Vedic name for Om or the God Shiva, who in the *Vedas* is also known as Rudra or the resounder, relating to the transformative power of the Divine Word. Om is called Tara or Taraka, the deliverer because, like a boat, it takes us across (tarati) the ocean of ignorance (Samsara). The main Sanskrit word for boat or ship (nau) also means the word (nau) and, as a feminine term, indicates Tara. Tara thus saves us from drowning or shipwreck, both literally and figuratively (being drowned by our emotional suffering in life).

As the power of deliverance Tara is related to the Goddess Durga, who similarly takes us across all difficulties (durgani). Hence she is also called Durga-Tara. Whereas Durga represents the power that overcomes or destroys obstacles and difficulties, Tara is the power which takes us beyond them. While Durga is more appropriate to call on in extreme danger wherein we need help against negative forces assailing us, Tara has the additional power to lift us up in life generally. Tara is the power to transcend all things. She not only lifts us beyond dangers but allows us to rise beyond our achievements and accomplishments to higher levels of realization. As the ultimate obstacle we have to cross over is our own mind, Tara provides the power to take us beyond the turbulent waves of our thought currents, which are nothing but a fragmentation of the sound current or Divine Word.

Tara is the feminine form of Om or Om personified as a Goddess. Tara is the unmanifest sound that exists in the ether of consciousness, through which we can go beyond the entire manifestation. Tara is Om that has the appearance of the ether and which pervades the ether as its underlying vibratory support, but also transcends it. Om is the unmanifest field behind creation, which is the destroyer as well as the creator of the universe.

Om as the Teacher or Guru

Om is the sound that reveals all other words and their different meanings. Om or the primal sound is the original ether behind all creation, but it is a little different than ether in the ordinary sense. Ether in the ordinary sense is just a medium. Om also has a luminous nature and reveals things.

According to Patanjali's *Yoga Sutras*, Om is the voice of Ishvara, the Lord, the primal world-guru. All his instructions come forth through Om. Hence we must first contact the power of Om for other mantras to work and for their specific meanings to be known. We must first contact Om to know the guru or Divine guiding power within us. Different mantras are only valuable as various means of integrating us back into the primal unitary sound vibration which is Om. Hence Om precedes all other mantras. Only through their connection with Om can other mantras be effective or be understood in their specific natures. As such, Tara contains within herself all mantras, and only through her grace can we come to understand and use them properly. Tara is perhaps the most important Goddess of mantric knowledge, the very personification of mantra Shakti.

The same Divine sound or primal root meaning enters into manifest sounds and affords them their particular meanings. Tara gives poetic and oratory powers to her devotees, and should be worshipped by those who seek these capacities. One devoted to Tara, it is said, can never be defeated in debate or in the display of literary talents.

SOUND AND BREATH

Tara is the purifying force of the vital breaths. Sound that manifests in the ether is the same as the Prana (life-force) that manifests in the ether. Breath is the primal sound of life, and the sound of the breath is the original, spontaneous and unuttered mantra (So'ham). Both mind and Prana, as word and vibration, have their root in sound. Hence the use of sound or mantra both purifies and energizes the mind.

TARA AS KNOWLEDGE

Tara is the radiance of knowledge that arises from the differentiation of meanings through sound. Different sounds serve as vehicles whereby different ideas or meanings flash forth. Om is the underlying light that illumines these different sounds and allows meaning to flow through them. All meanings exist to reintegrate us into the ocean of meaning that is pure consciousness itself.

Tara is thus of the nature of knowledge and inquiry into crossing over Samsara or the waters of darkness. All knowledge is a striving towards the infinite and the eternal, an attempt to link us back to some greater reality. This inherent aspiration of Tara hidden in our speech and our thought is ever seeking to move us beyond the realm of the known.

Tara relates specifically to the third of the four stages of speech, Pashyanti, the state of seeing, the perceptive or illumined word. She is sound that perceives or reveals the truth. Knowledge and perception are thus not different than subtle sound. For the perfection of true knowledge, Tara should be worshipped. Tara is the Goddess of consciousness itself.

TARA AS SPEECH

In her manifest form Tara is the consort (Shakti) of Brihaspati or Jupiter, the Vedic lord of wisdom, who is the Lord of manifest sound.

As the abode of speech, Tara relates to the tongue. In Sanskrit, tongue (jihva) is a feminine term. On a mystic level the tongues are the tongues of fire (Agni) or the speech powers of the Cosmic Being (Purusha). Tara is not only the power of speech but the ability to discern the taste or flavor of things, the esthetic mind. She allows us to perceive the essence in all things, which is perfect delight (ananda). She helps the Soma or immortal nectar flow into us. As such she is connected with Soma or the Moon and with the esoteric (yogic), as opposed to the exoteric (ritualistic) path (represented by Jupiter).

In Puranic mythology, Tara (the stars) is the wife of Jupiter, but also has a secret love affair with the Moon. Tara thus has a dual nature, both supporting knowledge (Jupiter) and ecstasy (the Moon). From her relationship with the Moon, she gives birth to a son, who is Mercury, the planet of speech and intelligence.

TARA AND GAURI

Tara, as a form of Kali, is another form of the consort of Lord Shiva. As such Tara is called Gauri, who is the wife of Shiva in her beneficent form. Gauri represents the Divine Mother in her nurturing capacity, which is her capacity to increase spiritual knowledge within us. She represents pure light and knowledge standing beyond all ignorance and duality. Tara takes us back to Gauri, the Divine Mother who stands behind all the worlds.

UGRA TARA/ NILA SARASVATI

Tara has a wrathful or terrible form, which is called Ugra or fierce Tara. In this capacity she is dark blue in color and is also called Nila (dark blue) Sarasvati, or the Goddess of speech. The wrathful form of Tara is thus also the wrathful form of Sarasvati, which is the protective and destructive power of speech. Ugra Sarasvati gives us victory in all debates and contests of knowledge, but for this we must be devoted to truth, not merely to our own opinions.

LOCATION IN THE BODY

Tara relates primarily to the Navel Chakra, which is the center for the third or illumined stage of speech (Pashyanti). Her other center is the tongue. Yet because she is the rising sound current that leaps upward from the navel center, she is not limited to this location. As Om or the guru she relates to the Third Eye or Ajña Chakra. She is thus the rising current from the Navel Chakra to the head.

MEDITATION FORM

Tara's meditation form is described as follows:

> *Mother, dark blue Saraswati, who grant all that is auspicious to those who surrender to you, who sit with your left leg extended, you who are the heart of Shiva, with a smiling lotus face,*
> *Who have three eyes like a budding lotus, the creatrix, who carry a severed head, a lotus, and a sword, I take refuge in you, the supreme lady of the worlds.*
> — Tarashtakam 1

Tara, like Kali, is deep blue in color. She has matted hair, wears a garland of human heads, and has eight serpents for her ornaments. She is dancing on a corpse, has four arms and carries in her four hands a sword or head chopper, a scissors, a severed head and a lotus.

Tara like Kali is dark blue (nila) according to her Tamasic nature. Tamas (darkness) is the nature of the unmanifest. As Kali is unmanifest time, Tara is unmanifest sound. From illumining the unitary nature of sound vibration (nada), she has matted hair. Her eight serpents relate to the eight siddhis (magic powers which gives us the ability to assume any size and shape and to fulfill any desire we might have). Her scissors relates to her ability to cut off all attachments. Her carrying a lotus flower symbolizes her open heart.

Tara is also portrayed as white, particularly as relating to Gauri, referring to her transcendent immaculate form. She is dark blue in her descent into creation. She is multicolored in action in the outer world. In Buddhist thought there are additional colors of Tara according to her different functions as the cosmic Mother (white, blue, yellow, red and green). These resemble not only Kali but also Lakshmi and Sarasvati, the Hindu Goddesses of beauty and wisdom.

MANTRA

Tara's main mantra, her bija or seed-syllable, is Om. She can be worshipped simply by chanting Om. She possesses a longer five syllable mantra:

Om hrīm strīm hūm phaṭ

Om is the mantra of deliverance (Taraka Mantra). Hrīm is a mantra of purification and transformation. Strīm is the feminine nature (stri) and provides the power to give birth and sustenance. Hūm is the mantra of Divine wrath and protection, as well as knowledge and perceptive power. Phat also gives protection and destroys obstacles.

This mantra has two variations. Either the initial Om can be dropped — hrīm strīm hūm phat — or both the initial Om and the concluding phat can be dropped — hrīm strīm hūm. The three forms of the mantra relate to the three aspects of the Mother as pure consciousness, as the cosmic ruler, and as the Kundalini or serpent power. Sometimes the second syllable is presented as trīm, which relates specifically to deliverance. Particularly in her wrathful role, Tara can be worshipped simply by the mantra hūm, which is a significant part of all variations on her mantra. The Tara Yantra can be used along with the mantra.

The seer of Tara's mantra is the Rishi Akshobhya. Akshobhya means without disturbance and he represents the aspect of Lord Shiva that transcends all agitation. He is also one of the five Dhyani or meditation Buddhas in the Buddhist tradition and symbolizes the mirror-like wisdom that reflects everything with detachment and which nothing can disturb. Only when the mind is free of agitation can we chant the mantra and gain its full power.

All people are entitled to use Om, which is called the Tara Vidya or knowledge relating to Tara. Om is not only for renunciates or for the initiated. It is the most universal and therefore most motherly of all mantras. It does not recognize any special outer requirements of class or age, nor any inner requirements of initiation, discipline or knowledge. It is the beginning and end of all the teachings, and hence can be freely used by everyone according to their aspirations.

MEDITATION APPROACHES

Tara's main meditational approach is through mantra, particularly repeating Om, which can be chanted along with the breath. While repeating mantras to Tara one should also call upon Divine grace to save and deliver all beings, and thereby become Tara oneself.

Another way to worship Tara is to let the mind abide in the interval of silence between manifest sounds — to try to hear the silence between sounds. The unmanifest sound Om exists in the interval between manifest sounds, but owing to our attachment to manifest sounds we fail to hear it. While repeating Om one should trace the root of thought, following the sound current back to its source in silence. All thought is a kind of sound vibration. At the root of all thought is Om or Tara, which takes us to our inner Self (Atman) that is pure silence. If we do this we will find the energy of our awareness naturally arising and ascending, lifting us effortlessly beyond all obstacles, dangers and attachments.

TRIPURA SUNDARI YANTRA

3

TRIPURA SUNDARI:
The Beauty of the Three Worlds

*Whose eyes are like a freshly-blooming lotus, who is
dark like an autumn rain cloud — we take refuge in the
wife of Lord Shiva, the three-eyed one, in Tripura Sundari,
the Goddess of the beauty of the three worlds.*

*Who dwells in a forest of bliss, whose ornaments
glisten with gold, who wears a great pearl necklace, whose
mouth rolls with wine, who is the giver of great compassion,*

*Who has wide eyes and wanders free — we take refuge
in the wife of the three-eyed one, in Tripura Sundari, the
Goddess of the beauty of the three worlds.*
                    —*Shankaracarya, Tripura Sundari Stotra*

THE BEAUTY OF PURE PERCEPTION

The feminine nature is synonymous with beauty. Examining the
cosmic manifestation we see that the female represents the Divine in form,
while the male represents the formless Divine. Yet what is beauty and
where does the highest beauty lie? Tantra asks us to search for the source
of beauty, and like the English poet Keats says that "beauty is truth and
truth is beauty." It says that the highest beauty is not on the outside but
on the inside. External beauty can only reflect for a moment a greater
internal beauty which transcends all forms. Sundari literally means
beauty. To worship her is to follow the path of beauty and delight through
the world of nature into the Absolute.

Normally we think of beauty as some perfection or harmony of form
and appearance, like a beautiful woman or a beautiful flower. Yet,
however beautiful anything may appear to be, if we look deeply we can
always find in it some flaw or imperfection. And whatever form of beauty
there is must pass away, often very quickly. Form may appear to possess
beauty but beauty is always more than any form. True beauty is eternal
and merely reflected onto the changing forms of things.

Sundari is not the ordinary beauty of form (which is more properly
an aspect of Kamala). The highest beauty does not lie in any object, though

TRIPURA SUNDARI

it is not apart from objects. The highest beauty is of perception — to "hold Infinity in the palm of your hand, and Eternity in an hour," as the poet Blake so eloquently wrote.

Beauty derives from the light of consciousness that is irradiated through objects. It is never really contained in any object. Hence beauty can never pass away but merely has manifold forms for its revelation. The light of beauty we see in things is thus the light of our own awareness. Discovering this we contact the well springs of infinite delight within us. This is part of the revelation of Sundari.

The beauty of perception occurs only when the mind is cleansed from the known, when consciousness is cleared of its conditioning and rests in pure awareness without any residue of memory. Then whatever we see is irradiated with the light of eternity and is effulgent with the glory of our own Self as the Universal Being. Otherwise the residue of our thoughts and emotions, like a dark film, obstructs the subtle and transparent beauty and presence in things, though we may be able to perceive clearly their physical characteristics.

Sundari represents the ultimate beauty of pure perception which arises when we see all the universe in ourselves, when we see all nature as a reflection of the reality of consciousness. Sundari is thus the beauty of nature but as seen through the spiritual eye of unity — the vision that all the universe is Brahman — that there is nothing but God above, below, within, without, to the north, south, east or west, past, present or future.

This is not to perceive some distant creator in a heaven beyond, but the revelation of our own eternal and infinite Self in every moment of perception. When the mind is permeated with such unlimited awareness it finds a plenary delight in every thing that we see. It finds perception to be joy, even if we are looking at the most ordinary things. Freed of the concepts of time and space, size, distance, and importance, each perception reveals the eternal presence and becomes a universe in itself. The mind thereby is stopped and enters Samadhi or the blissful state.

THE GODDESS OF VEDANTIC KNOWLEDGE

Sundari thus is the Goddess of Vedantic knowledge, which is the knowledge of the Supreme Self or Divine I Am. She teaches us that all is the Self and that the world is Brahman or the Absolute. From her perspective Samsara is Nirvana; the world of illusion is merged into the Absolute. Hence she is the form of the Goddess most beloved among Vedantic Swamis and teachers. She represents the knowledge of the Supreme Self.

TRIPURA, THE THREE CITIES

Sundari is called Tripura or "of the three cities." Pura means cities; Tri means three. The three cities are the three worlds and our three bodies through which we experience them — the physical, astral, and causal, or matter, energy, and thought. These correspond to the three states of consciousness: waking, dream, and deep sleep. They are symbolized by the three lights of fire, moon and sun. The being who delights in these three world experiences, yet inherently transcends them, is Tripura Sundari.

Her first city is the waking state wherein our consciousness dwells in the eye (the senses). Her second city is the dream state, which occurs in the Throat Chakra, wherein our consciousness dwells in the mind. Her third city is deep sleep, which occurs in the heart, wherein our consciousness returns to its true nature. As the ruler of the three, Sundari is the mystic fourth, the state of Turiya or Samadhi.

LALITA, SHE WHO PLAYS

Sundari is called Lalita or "she who plays." The entire universe exists for the delight of awareness, which is the play of the Divine Mother. Creation arises in joy, abides in joy, and returns to joy. We are but transient figures in her eternal play, who have yet to understand the source of the energy that moves us. Our sorrow and suffering is a delusion, a misconception born of ignorance and the ego. Because we attempt to control or possess joy from the standpoint of the separate self, we divide ourselves from true joy which is universal. The Goddess, as the image of joy, shows us the way out of our error, which is not to deny ourselves happiness but to discover the true happiness that we seek, which is in being one with all. Lalita awakens the receptive soul to the bliss that underlies all things.

Lalita is the deity of the Shri Chakra, the great yantra or energy pattern which underlies the entire universe, which arises from the mantra Om. She is the most blissful and beautiful of all the Goddesses, as she represents the ultimate bliss at the source of all delights. She is the deity who dwells at the summit of Mount Meru, the cosmic mountain or the mountain of the spine, and gives the orders whereby the entire universe moves. She is the Divine love which is the central motivating force behind the universe, and which is the original impulse within our own hearts.

RAJARAJESHVARI,
THE SUPREME RULER OF THE UNIVERSE

Sundari is also called Rajarajeshvari or "the supreme ruler of the universe." From her arise all the commands which govern the universe, including the command which allows us to unfold spiritually or to give spiritual teachings in the world. We must seek her command in order to do anything significant in life. Yet her command is not based on authority but love. To gain her approval we merely need be open to her love. What she allows us to do is to love her and to love everything. To discover her commands, however, we must be willing to surrender our own egoistic desires and attempts to control things.

Beauty and bliss is the fundamental energy of existence, and play is the nature of all manifestation. Knowing this we can easily free ourselves from attachment and find happiness and delight in whatever life may bring us. This insight is part of the knowledge of Sundari.

SUNDARI AS A YOUNG GIRL

Tripura Sundari is often represented as a young girl of sixteen years age. As such she is called "sixteen" (shodasi) or "the young girl" (bala). At this stage of a woman's life the delight aspect of her existence is most pronounced. Her nature is to play, to seek new experience, and to charm others to her. Her innocence attracts to her all that is true and good.

As a young girl Sundari guides the young aspirant on the path, representing the innocence of initial aspiration that we should preserve throughout our entire journeying into the infinite.

SUNDARI AS KNOWLEDGE AND CONSCIOUSNESS

Sundari is the power of consciousness, Cit-shakti. She is the awareness of the Supreme Self, Paramatman, as one with the Supreme Reality or Absolute, Parabrahman. As true knowledge she is called Samvit, which is the power to comprehend all things as consciousness itself.

Sundari is thus the power of spiritual knowledge (jñana-shakti), which is more a matter of feeling and perception than of thought and analysis. Hence she is the form of the Goddess most to be worshipped by those following the Yoga of Knowledge. She is the form of the Goddess who most represents pure consciousness and the bliss that flows from it. She combines the being of Kali, with the knowledge of Tara and adds the bliss dimension of spiritual realization.

SOMA AND THE MOON

Sundari represents the Moon as the visible image of delight. This nectar of the Moon or the mind intoxicated by Divine beauty is called Soma in the *Vedas*. Sundari is the experience of the flowing Soma or nectar-bliss. In this regard she represents the delight of the Divine Self as he consumes our mind (Moon) and digests all experiences as pure joy.

LOCATION IN THE BODY

Sundari is the deity of the Crown Chakra or thousand-petalled lotus, the abode of the immortal nectar (amrit). By her grace the nectar descends and comes to pervade the entire body, until we find the entire universe dwelling within it.

MEDITATION FORM

Sundari has the complexion of the rising sun and wears a crescent moon on her crown, which is sometimes figured as made up of her own matted hair. She has four arms, and carries in two hands a sugar cane bow and five flower arrows, and in the other two a noose and a hook. She is often portrayed as naked yet with all adornments (bracelets, armlets, anklets, earrings, rings and necklaces). She is young and beautiful and is generally shown as sitting on a cot, which is itself the reclining deity Sadashiva, on top of the four forms of Brahma, Vishnu, Rudra, and Maheshvara, who are the legs of a cot.

Her rosy complexion indicates her joy, illumination and compassion. The mind is her sugar-cane bow and the five senses her arrows, which under her power of awareness become instruments of bliss. Sundari shoots us with the arrows of delight, revealing all the forms of creation as aspects of our own blissful nature of pure consciousness. Her noose indicates her ability to capture her devotees with her beauty. Her hook cuts off all attachment to outer appearances.

The five forms of Shiva that she sits on are called the five corpses as they are inert without her energy. They symbolize the five elements and the fivefold act of Shiva. Brahma is element of earth and the act of creation. Vishnu is water and preservation. Rudra is fire and destruction. Maheshvara is air and the basic ignorance or act of concealment which allows the world to manifest in consciousness. Sadashiva is ether and liberation, whereby we transcend the world and whereby the Divine withdraws the world into itself.

MANTRA

Sundari's mantra is the famous Pañchadashi or fifteen syllable mantra of Sri Vidya. It has three sections (kutas), each ending with the mantra Hrīm, which mantra by itself can be used to worship Sundari or Lalita (see the explication of this mantra under Bhuvaneshvari).

Ka e ī la	hrīm
Ka sa ka ha la	hrīm
Sa ka la	hrīm

This mantra has many variations. Ending it with the mantra Shrīm makes it the sixteen fold (shodasi) mantra. The fifteen are said to be the digits of the Moon, which waxes and wanes during the lunar month. The sixteenth is the eternal essence. The sixteen are also the sixteen vowels of the Sanskrit alphabet.

The first set of mantras is said to be the head of the Goddess, the second from her neck to her hips, and the third the region below the hips. The first set relates to Vak, the power of speech, the second to Kamaraja, the king of love, and the third to the original Shakti or power of transformation. These three sections also relate to Brahma, Vishnu and Shiva, to the three *Vedas* (*Rig, Yajur,* and *Sama*).

There are many ways to explain this mantra. Whole books have been written on it. Below is a short examination of its syllables. Relative to the first of the three sections of the mantra: Ka is desire or the creator. E is Maya or the power of illusion. I is Vishnu or the Divine ruling power. La is the power of bliss.

Relative to the second section: Ha is space or breath. Sa is time. Ka again is creation. Ha is breath or spirit renewed in energy. La again is bliss.

Relative to the third section: Sa is time as eternity or totality. Ka is origin and also the unknown. La again is bliss.

Hrīm repeated three times brings about a triple transformation of our nature. Srīm added at the end is the crowning glory and realization.

As Bala, a beautiful girl of sixteen, Sundari is worshipped by the mantra Aim klīm sauh. Aim is the power of wisdom. Klīm is the power of beauty and delight. Sauh is the power of transformation and transcendence.

The seer of Sundari's mantra is Shiva Dakshinamurti, the silent sage of sixteen years of age who, seated below the sacred fig tree, teaches his disciples, many of whom are old men, and clears all their doubts without uttering a word. He represents the highest spiritual knowledge and thus affirms the inner meaning of Sundari as the Bliss of Self-realization. He is also the form of Shiva who rules the Sri Chakra. The Sri Chakra itself can be used as the yantra for worshipping Sundari (or any of the Dasha Mahavidya), or the specific Sundari Yantra can be employed.

Shiva Dakshinamurti should be worshipped by all those who seek initiation into this mantra or into any mantras. He holds the key to all wisdom, both mantric and meditational. If one does not have a guru, one can initiate oneself into a mantra before an image of Dakshinamurti. If the aspirant is sincere Dakshinamurti himself will energize the mantra for him. The modern sage said to be Dakshinamurti incarnate was Bhagavan Ramana Maharshi.

Sundari is the feminine of Sundara, the bliss form of Shiva. Sundara is Shiva as the wooer of the Goddess as Parvati, the daughter of the mountain. Wherever there is Shiva or peace, there must be Sundara or beauty. Similarly, wherever there is Sundari or the beauty of perception, there must be Shiva or peace of mind.

MEDITATION APPROACHES

To be aware of the Divine beauty in all things is the way to approach Sundari. This requires that we purify our perception. To cleanse the mind of thought and to merge the seer into the seen is her way of knowledge.

The highest worship of Sundari is to abide in the Self, to be who we really are, the Self of the entire universe. In abiding in our true nature is the vision of all the universe as Brahman. When the seer (fire or Agni) unites with the seen (Soma), then the essence or nectar of the seen comes out as bliss. This is the Yoga of Sundari.

The main method for this is Self-inquiry (Atma-vichara) whereby we trace the root of the I thought to its origin in the consciousness of the universal Self. Then we come to experience that all things are not different from ourselves and in that experience find the supreme delight.

Another important way to worship Sundari is to meditate upon the great sayings (Mahavakya) of Vedanta. Most important are Aham Brahmasmi or "I am Brahman (the Absolute)" and Sarvakhalvidam Brahman or "Everything is Brahman." It is not enough merely to think about these statements. One must feel them with one's entire being. They are the great attitudes that we must cultivate.

According to this summit view of Vedanta, it is beneath our dignity as the Supreme Self to bow down before any fear, worry, sorrow, anxiety or other pettiness of mind. It is beneath our Divine status as universal Awareness to identify with some minuscule body or mind or world somewhere. It is similarly an insult to the Self in others to regard them as limited to a body or in need of help, upliftment, or consolation. Such attitudes give us the grace of Sundari whereby we perceive the bliss of Brahman everywhere and help it to come forth.

The worship of Sri Chakra is another important way to worship Sundari. This requires understanding all the aspects of the Yantra and all of its various mantras and deities. This would also require a book in itself to examine.

RAMANA MAHARSHI AND ANANDAMAYI MA

The great modern seer of the Sundari Vidya is Bhagavan Ramana Maharshi, who ever abided in the bliss of pure seeing which is the Self of all beings. The great modern incarnation of Sundari was Shri Anandamayi Ma (1896–1982), the bliss-permeated Mother of Bengal, perhaps the most famous and widely-venerated woman teacher of modern India. Ma constantly laughed from the state of Divine bliss, transcending all the dualities of the phenomenal world. Another way to worship Sundari is to worship Ma.

BHUVANESHVARI YANTRA

4
BHUVANESHVARI:
The Queen of the Universe

Of the myriad thousands of Shaktis who, containing all accomplished powers, play in the three worlds, Bhuvaneshvari, Queen of the worlds, you have the power of vision behind all their consummate manifold powers, as the creator, preserver and destroyer of the universe.
— Ganapati Muni, Uma Sahasram 7.3

Bhuvaneshvari means the Queen or ruler (feminine, Ishvari) of the universe or realm of being (Bhuvana). She is the Divine Mother as the Queen of all the worlds. All the universe is her body and all beings are ornaments on her infinite being. She carries all the worlds as a flowering of her own Self-nature. She is thus related to Sundari and to Rajarajeshvari, the supreme Lady of the universe.

THE GODDESS AS SPACE

Bhuvaneshvari is known in the *Vedas* as Aditi, the infinite or indivisible Mother, the great origin and cosmic womb, who is space. In her as genesis and origin all light is born. Hence she is the Mother of the Sun and all the Sun Gods who are named after her (Adityas). The Mother creates space in order to give birth to all things. Similarly she creates space within our own consciousness to give birth to the Divine nature within us.

Space has many levels of manifestation. There is not only the space of the physical universe but also the space of the mind. Just as the outer or world space is infinite, so is the inner or mind space. There are many additional layers of space in the higher levels of the mind. Ultimately, there is the supreme space of pure consciousness beyond all manifestation. All of these are aspects and functions of Bhuvaneshvari.

In the microcosm, our own body, the entire universe is contained in the small space that dwells within the heart. The heart is where the infinite space hides within us, and is the real seat of the Divine Mother.

The Goddess represents space. Space is the Mother or matrix in which all creatures come into being. She is the field in which all things grow.

BHUVANESHVARI

She is the receptive spirit who gives space to allow all things their place and function. She is the cosmic womb that gives birth to all the worlds.

As space, Bhuvaneshvari is complementary to Kali who is time; they are the two main faces of the Goddess as both the infinite and the eternal. Bhuvaneshvari creates the stage on which Kali performs her dance of life and death. As the stage Bhuvaneshvari is also the witness, the observer and the enjoyer of the dance.

The Goddess as Place and Direction

As Kali creates events in time, so Bhuvaneshvari creates objects in space. All events are merely episodes in the Divine Mother Kali who is time. All places are merely phases of the dance of the Divine Mother Bhuvaneshvari who is space. The Goddess is the place, the field, the matrix in which we act to manifest the Gods. Knowing her as the ground on which we stand and the reality which pervades us, we gain the capacity (Shakti) to accomplish the highest actions, which are the practices of Yoga. Returning to her passive presence, we ourselves become the field in which the Gods, the cosmic powers, can be born and assume their roles in the cosmic creative unfoldment.

Bhuvaneshvari represents the directions of space. The four directions of north, south, east and west are the different views of her presence and each has its specific quality. Kali similarly creates the directions of time, which are past, present and future. Yet space also reflects an unfoldment in time. East represents the beginning, while north is the direction of enlightenment. West represents maturation, while south is the region of completion. Hence space contains time. Similarly, time is space and each time has its location, direction and orientation.

Place is only a reflection of our vision: as moves our vision, so moves the place in which we appear to be. Vision moreover determines our direction. As we direct our minds, so do we perceive certain places or events. Bhuvaneshvari thus represents the original creative vision of the supreme, the direction of his attention or force of awareness.

The Goddess as Primal Matter

Space is the primal matter which is the root of all the elements. The gross elements, like earth and water, are merely densified or concentrated space, as modern physics has revealed. As the root substance of the universe the Goddess is called Prakriti, the primal substance, or Great Nature. We all live and move within the substance of the Goddess who is Bhuvaneshvari, who is Mother Nature personified. This primal space is consciousness and hence cannot disturb or weigh us down, but is the very expression of freedom and joy.

THE GODDESS OF THE UNIVERSE

Bhuvaneshvari is the cosmos (Bhuvana) personified as a Goddess. To worship her promotes a cosmic vision and frees us from the narrowness of opinion and belief. She helps us go beyond all identifications with creed, class, race, sex, nation and religion, to a universal understanding. She gives us world vision, a global understanding, and a sense of the infinite. Hence she is a very important Goddess in the present day wherein we need to create a global culture and get beyond the divisive beliefs which are destroying the planet.

MAYA

As the power that measures out the universe, Bhuvaneshvari is called Maya, which also means illusion. When things are measured we can become caught in their limited forms and forget the underlying unitary space in which they appear. This is how illusion arises. All manifest forms are merely waves in the infinite space of the Divine Mother. We must learn to see the space of the Mother, which is the embrace of consciousness, in all the apparent objects of the world, and no longer take their diverse forms as reality. Consciousness is the field in which all objects occur and without which they have no meaning. Grasping that field we can possess all objects, the entire universe itself, without leaving the room in which we are meditating.

AS THE POWER OF LOVE

As Kali is the power of action (kriya-shakti) and Sundari is the power of knowledge (jnana-shakti), so Bhuvaneshvari is the power of love (iccha-shakti). Love creates space and gives freedom. It does not limit or try to possess, which is the action of selfish desire. Yet the space of love is not an empty or unfriendly space, it is a space that nurtures and gives room to grow and flower. If love does not give space, it is not a Divine love and not yet mature. Such a limited love only serves to smother us in attachment and suffering. The love of Bhuvaneshvari breaks us free of these bonds by making us aware that true love has no form and all forms, and that to truly love is to love space and consciousness and not to be attached to mere things and appearances.

Love or Divine desire (iccha) results in the desire to create or envision (iksha). Bhuvaneshvari is the power of love that envisions the universe as creative play. Space is never without energy. When space is created, a power (shakti) must come forth in it as vision and action. Hence the universe arose inevitably from the infinite space of consciousness. Those who wish to be great artists, visionaries and creators should worship Bhuvaneshvari and first create her sacred space within their own minds.

AS PEACE

Space is peace, rest, repose and perfect equanimity. By creating space we release ourselves from stress and tension, which are forms of narrowness, reaction and attachment. This is part of the grace of the Goddess Bhuvaneshvari. Those seeking the supreme peace should worship Bhuvaneshvari. Bhuvaneshvari is the power of infinite wideness, equanimity and peace that has the power to bear all things and which can be stained or disturbed by nothing.

AS THE VOID

Bhuvaneshvari represents the Void or original space in which things come into being. She is the Void in its creative form, the void within creation, from which creation springs and which supports the unfoldment of further creation. She is not the void that is prior to and beyond creation (which is Dhumavati).

LOCATION IN THE BODY

Bhuvaneshvari is located in all space. As such we are always in Bhuvaneshvari. But above all she is the space within the heart in which all the universe is contained. This is not merely the Heart Chakra but the heart center on the right side of the chest, which is the seat of Self-awareness. In this regard Bhuvaneshvari or the Queen of the Universe is always within us.

MEDITATION FORM

Bhuvaneshvari has a form like Sundari, whom she resembles in many ways, which reveals her beneficent nature. She has the color of the rising sun, with the crescent moon on her head, with four hands and three eyes. She holds in two hands the noose and the goad. With her other two hands she gives the gestures that grant boons and dispel fears. Sometimes she is shown carrying a lotus and a pot of jewels in two of her hands, or her left foot is placed upon a pot of jewels. She is seated on a couch-like throne, which consists of the five forms of Shiva (as described under Sundari), from which she directs all the movements in the universe. She is surrounded by various attendant deities, Gods and Goddesses, who enact her commands from her place of serenity.

MANTRA

The mantra for Bhuvaneshvari is the single syllable Hrīm. Hrīm is one of the most important of all mantras. It is called the Devi Pranava, or the equivalent of Om for the Goddess. Hrīm refers to the heart (Hridaya). It also relates to Hri, which is modesty.

The mantra Hrīm is the general mantra of Shiva's consort and of Maheshvari, the supreme Goddess. It can be used for all the Ten Wisdom Goddesses, and as the main mantra of the Sri Chakra is commonly used for Sundari. It is a single syllable easy for anyone to use. The *Devi Gita* states (XII.28):

> *All my worship can be performed with the mantra Hrim. Of all mantras, Hrim is regarded as the supreme guide.*

Bhuvaneshvari as the Mother can be worshipped through the mantra Mā, which is the natural sound for mother. This mantra, like Hrīm, can be used for the Divine Mother in all her forms. The Divine Mother is called Shrī Mā (respected, beautiful or resplendent Mother), which can also be used as a mantra for her.

The seer of her mantra is Shiva as Bhuvaneshvara, the Lord of the world, or Nataraj, the Lord of the Dance which is the universe. Bhuvaneshvari also dances and her dance becomes all creation. Relative to yantras, Bhuvaneshvari can be worshipped by the Shri Yantra or Bhuvaneshvari Yantra.

MEDITATION APPROACHES

One approaches Bhuvaneshvari by meditating upon infinite space or the void. To arrive at this some practical and intermediate methods can be helpful. One such method is to concentrate on the space between objects rather than on the objects themselves. Everywhere there is space containing objects but usually we see the objects and miss the space. Yet that space is the Divine presence and, if we give attention to it, it connects us with the love and peace of the Divine Mother.

Another method of her knowledge is to cultivate the attitude of the witness, wherein one merely observes but does not identify with anything, as if one were like space, present but not affected by anything. Within each of us is a certain portion of our nature that is indeed like a witness, never affected by anything, and inherently beyond suffering. This is our portion of Bhuvaneshvari.

Yet another method is to dwell on the unknown and cease to recognize names and forms as a reality. All that we know is really an imposition of name and form on an unknown, ungraspable presence which resembles the void, yet is alive and teeming with energy.

To gain the creative force of Bhuvaneshvari we should hold all our creative energy inside ourselves, offering it inwardly to the Goddess, so that she can form it in whichever way she wishes. To become empty, motiveless and open before truth is to honor her.

BHAIRAVI YANTRA

5
BHAIRAVI:
The Warrior Goddess

She who has color of the Fire, effulgent with the power of Tapas blazing, the one who is desired in the fruits of all actions, I take refuge in her, the Goddess Durga. Reverence to the wonderful savioress for our deliverance.

Fire, deliver us anew, across all difficulties to wellbeing. Be a wide, vast and abundant city for us, as peace and happiness for all the progeny of our creative work.

Fire, Knower of all births, as a ship across the sea, deliver us across all difficulties. Like the Sun, chanting with the mind, awaken as the protector of our being.
— *Mahanarayana Upanishad, Durga Sukta 2–4*

According to the Zuni Indians of North America, all spiritual phenomena falls into two categories: the beautiful and the dangerous. These are not mutually exclusive. The beautiful and the terrible often go together, as we have already noted under the figure of Kali. Bhairavi specifically means "terrifying" and is the powerful, awesome, or energetic form of the Goddess. She represents transforming heat or radiance, Tejas, which is the primal power or Divine energy. This we experience as a frightening thing because it burns away and destroys all the limitations and illusions of egocentric existence.

Bhairavi represents Divine anger and wrath. Yet her wrath is directed toward the impurities within us, as well as to the negative forces that may try to interfere with our spiritual growth. Though a difficult force to bear, her activity is necessary both to guide and to protect us. Bhairavi is the proverbial wrath of a woman and more specifically the wrath of a mother toward whatever may threaten her children.

BHAIRAVI AS THE SUPREME GODDESS OF SPEECH
Bhairavi represents the supreme power of speech, which has the nature of fire (Tejas). She is the Word in its unarticulated and primal form as raw energy, the flaming word which appears like a pillar or a sword to

BHAIRAVI

remove all opposition. She is the supreme light and heat power, the flame of consciousness itself (Cidagni) which is the ultimate knowledge of truth.

Bhairavi as Tejas (radiance) rules over the Tanmatras, the subtle sensory potentials behind the five elements and five sense organs which allow for their interconnection. Through the Tanmatras Bhairavi gives power over the senses and the elements. She is the basic will power of life, mastering which we come to control all of its manifestations.

Bhairavi is known as Durga, the Goddess who saves us from difficulties. Durga rides a lion, a symbol of fire or solar energy, from which she wields her weapons of light to destroy all demons or negative forces. She helps take us beyond disease, sorrow, darkness and death.

Bhairavi is also related to Tara (the savioress). Both Bhairavi and Tara represent speech (Vak). However, while Tara represents the illumined Word (Pashyanti Vak), Bhairavi indicates the supreme Word (Para Vak). Hence Bhairavi is subtler than and is the origin of Tara. It could be said that the highest energization of speech as Tara becomes Bhairavi; the illumined Word turns into the supreme Light and heat. Conversely, it could be said that the original unarticulated flaming word (Bhairavi) takes shape and a human appearance through Tara.

BHAIRAVI AS TAPAS

The fierce form of Divine energy exists within us as the power of transforming heat (Tapas). Tapas is sometimes translated as asceticism. More properly it is a heightened aspiration that consumes all secondary interests and attachments. When we are really interested in something we naturally lose our attraction to other things. Tapas is this real interest and profound absorption in the spiritual life that causes us to no longer want anything else. Tapas is the heat of spiritual inquiry and aspiration which causes us to discard all that is non-essential in life.

Bhairavi as Tapas is especially worshipped by those seeking knowledge or by those seeking control of their sexual energy (Brahmacharya). She gives control of the senses, the emotions and wandering thoughts. She helps us during fasting, vows of silence, meditation retreats, pilgrimages, during the practice of celibacy, or any other concentrated spiritual discipline (Tapas) that we may be attempting. Whatever obstructions arise to our practice of Tapas we can call on Bhairavi to help eliminate them.

BHAIRAVI AS THE WOMAN WARRIOR

Bhairavi is the fierce form of the Goddess and related to Chandi, the fiercest form of the Goddess, who is the main deity of the famous *Devi Mahatmya*, a great poem of seven hundred verses (also called *Durga*

Saptasati or *Chandi*) which celebrates the destruction of the demons by her. Bhairavi is the woman as warrior, who with her power of Divine speech and spiritual fire eliminates all obstacles to the unfoldment of true awareness. As Chandi or the destroyer of opposition, she can be invoked for removing obstacles to allow us to attain any of the four goals of life — enjoyment, wealth, recognition or liberation (kama, artha, dharma and moksha).

Another important form of Durga is the ten-armed Mahishasura Mardini, the destroyer of Mahishasura, the demon who represents the vital passions (particularly sexual desires), which tie us to the outer world. She is also a form of Bhairavi.

THE THREE FORMS OF BHAIRAVI

Bhairavi, like Sundari, is Tripura or "of the three worlds," yet while Sundari is the beauty, Bhairavi is the terror. Beauty and terror are complementary. In the Tantric path we move from terror to beauty. We must endure the transforming heat and light of Bhairavi before we can enjoy the cool and gentle bliss of Sundari.

Bhairavi is threefold as Fire (Agni), Lightning (Vidyut), and the Sun (Surya). These are her three light forms in the three worlds of Earth, Atmosphere and Heaven. Her earthly form is primary, as it is in the Earthly sphere that the warrior power is most needed.

The three great demon-slaying forms of the Goddess worshipped in the *Devi Mahatmya*, are also her forms. These are Mahalakshmi, Mahakali, and Mahasarasvati, the great (maha) forms of Lakshmi, the consort of Vishnu, the preserver; Kali the consort of Shiva, the destroyer; and Sarasvati the consort of Brahma, the creator. These are the great forms of the Goddess as destroyers of all obstructions and negativity. Hence Bhairavi can be worshipped as the supreme form of the Goddess in her manifold forms.

BHAIRAVA AND RUDRA

Bhairavi's consort is Bhairava, the fierce form of Shiva. Bhairava is known as Rudra, the howler, the ancient Vedic deity from which Shiva arose. Shiva is the peace that follows the experience of the Divine wrath of Rudra which causes us to put our lives in order. Rudra represents the awesome power of the Divine Word. As his consort, Bhairavi is known as Rudrani. The worship of Rudra through the chant of the Rudram (a chapter of the *Yajur Veda*) relates to Bhairari.

Bhairavi is thus an awesome force that we should not try to arouse unless we are ready. We cannot accept her energy half-way, or take from her only what we want. We should only seek her grace if we are willing to undergo the fire-sacrifice of our own minds into the Divine.

LOCATION IN THE BODY

Bhairavi dwells at the base of the spine in the Root Chakra (muladhara). She is the same as Kundalini, most specifically in her awakened role as the purifier of our nature. Unless we are ready to deal with Bhairavi we should not try to arouse the Kundalini into action.

MEDITATION FORM

Bhairavi possesses the effulgence of a thousand rising suns. She has three eyes and wears a jeweled crown with the crest of the moon. Her lotus face is happy and smiling. She wears a red garment (generally made of silk), her breasts are smeared with blood, and she is adorned with a garland of severed human heads. She has four hands and carries a rosary and a book. She makes the gestures of knowledge and that for giving boons with the other two hands. Sometimes instead of the gesture of knowledge she makes the gesture of dispelling fear. She is seated on a red lotus or, in other depictions of her, on a corpse. The chief characteristic of her form is blazing light.

Bhairavi is the personification of light and fire, and represents the victory of the light. Hence she carries no weapons. She is the Goddess returning from her destruction of all demons or negative forces.

MANTRA

Bhairavi's mantra consists of three seed-syllables:

Hsraim hsklrīm hssrauḥ

This mantra has the power to uncover and destroy all negativity. It is a very forceful mantra that probes into our psyches and reveals the negative energies hidden within, totally uproots them and annihilates them. It is like a flaming torch aimed into the hidden corners of the mind to clear out any secret darkness within us. Hence it should be used with care and discretion. Hs is a hissing sound that causes the inner serpent power or Kundalini fire energy to move. Hsr is a particularly fiery and penetrating sound.

Brahma, Vishnu and Shiva are all three together said to be the seer of the mantra for Tripura Bhairavi, as in her three forms she is Mahasarasvati, Mahalakshmi and Mahakali, their consorts. Yet more specifically, Bhairava or the wrathful form of Shiva is her seer. The Bhairavi Yantra can also be used along with the mantra.

Bhairavi can also be worshipped by the mantra Svāhā, meaning self-offering, which is the main mantra by which offerings are made into the sacred Fire. Svāhā is one of the wives of Agni or the Divine Fire. Many mantras end with Svāhā as it gives them the power of the Supreme Word.

As Tripura, Bhairavi can be worshipped by the Pañcadashi Mantra for Tripura Sundari as listed above and through the Shri Chakra. However, in her case it is the wrathful energy of the Goddess that is meditated upon. To get to Sundari we must first pass through Bhairavi. The path of Yoga is from Bhairavi or the fierce form of the Goddess at the Root Chakra to Sundari or her blissful form at the Crown Chakra. This is also the way up the cosmic mountain or Shri Chakra.

MEDITATION APPROACHES

Meditation on the inner light is one means of approaching Bhairavi. This inner light is experienced through the Third Eye. Yet the inner light and inner sound go together. This inner sound is called Nada, which is the primal sound vibration before the arising of specific words. Contacting the flaming vibration at the root of the mind is communion with Bhairavi.

Tapas is another way to worship her. It is said that without Tapas (concentrated energy) nothing can be gained on the spiritual path. Hence the aspirant should regularly consecrate some offering to the Goddess, preferably of some aspect of his or her own nature, like relinquishing some desire, attachment, or pleasure. The highest Tapas is to control one's thoughts or silence the mind. Hence offering our thoughts into the flame of Awareness is a way to honor the Goddess. Another way is to offer our thoughts into the mantra by always returning our minds back to attention on it.

The outer form of worship for Bhairavi is Homa or the Vedic fire sacrifice (havana). Yet this can also be used as an inner form of worship. For this we must offer all our thoughts and emotions into the fire of the Divine Word which dwells in the root chakra. This is to withdraw the mind from the senses and sink it into the deepest part of our being. It is to let our speech sink from the throat to the base of the spine to merge into the light of silence.

CHHINNAMASTA YANTRA

6

CHHINNAMASTA:

The Consciousness Beyond the Mind

Her hands have no arms, her mouth has no face. She is the eye of the blind, Mother Prachanda Chandika.

Without a hand she fashions, she knows without a mind, without an eye she sees, Mother Prachanda Chandika.

She is the supreme hand of the hand, the wonderful consciousness of the mind, the eye that is the origin of the eye, Mother Prachanda Chandika.

Though her head is cut off, she is the support of life. Though she is frightening in appearance, she is the giver of peace. Though a maiden she increases our vigor, Mother Prachanda Chandika.

— *Ganapati Muni, Prachanda Chandika 9–11, 14*

THE IMAGE OF THE SEVERED HEAD:
GOING BEYOND THE MIND

One of the more fearful imaginings we can have in life is that of encountering a headless ghost or demon. Our inclination is not to give a spiritual meaning to such a fantasy but to see it as something macabre, a sign of neurosis. Yet what we are really afraid of in the image of a headless entity is the unreality of our own identity as an embodied being. To lose one's head over something is a common expression for becoming totally engrossed in something to the extent that we lose our ordinary sense of reality. To be without a head is a yogic metaphor for going beyond body consciousness or attachment to the thought-composed mind. The spiritual path is aimed at opening the lid of the mind so that we can have access to the universal consciousness beyond thought.

Actually we don't really see our head any more than we see the back of our body. We experience the inside of our head primarily as an open space. Hence we really don't have a head, except to the extent that we imagine our bodily form from our mirror image. According to the science of Yoga this headless state is our true reality as a conscious perceiver. Our location in the body is an illusory appearance, not a fundamental reality.

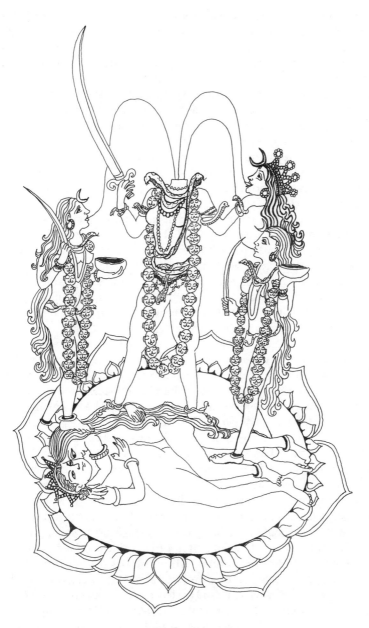

CHHINNAMASTA

It is a fixation of thought. If we do not sustain the "I-am-the-body" idea through constant thought, our consciousness will naturally return to its original, bodiless, thought-free state. This idea of having no head is emphasized in many teachings of the Yoga of Knowledge, including Chan and Zen teachings as well as Advaita Vedanta.

Chhinnamasta, whose image is a severed head, is the Goddess who causes us to cut off our own heads or to dissolve our minds into pure awareness. She brings transcendence of the mind and represents the non-mind (unmana) state. Freed from the limitations of the mind, consciousness realizes its true nature beyond death and sorrow.

Hence we need not fear losing our bodies or losing our heads. They are mere restrictions on our deeper reality. Death will take them anyway, regardless of what we may do. In fact the only way to real awareness is to sacrifice the mind, to give up the thought mechanism based on the self-image or the I-am-the-body idea. This mind sacrifice is symbolized by the cutting off of the head. It indicates the discrimination of the mind from the body, the freeing of consciousness from the shackles of body consciousness. Once this is done our consciousness will no longer be confined within the body. We will be free to experience the unity of our consciousness with all that we see, opening to the space of the infinite both above and behind the body will open up.

In addition, once the veil of the mind is lifted there will be the liberation of the subtle energies hidden within the body, which can then move upward and connect with the cosmic energy. The body will become a pillar of light streaming up into the infinite. The energies of the subtle body will become activated within the gross physical body, linking us up to the unmanifest state of pure awareness.

Yet we may ask, why should we portray this state in so graphic an image, when it can be conveyed more calmly via conceptual description? The image has a stronger and more dramatic impact on our psyche and conveys the process as fact rather than as theory. The mind can take in any theory and thereby avoid the reality. The image, however, cannot be so easily subverted. It communicates to the core of our being.

Moreover, should we actually experience this process, it is hardly a matter of philosophical thinking. It is a frightening and even physically painful (though liberating process) which removes us permanently from the realm of ordinary human experience. Even the initial stages of this process can cause much doubt and anxiety as we see our ordinary identity taken away from us. The pain of the ego-sacrifice is something that no one wants to experience, even once we recognize its necessity. It causes a total reorientation of our energies which is like being reborn. Such a dramatic image is appropriate to what is the most transformative experience possible for us.

The Severed Head as Liberation

Chhinnamasta — which literally means "a severed head" — is perhaps the most frightening or disturbing form of the Goddess. She has cut off her own head and, holding it in her right hand, with it drinks the blood flowing from her own severed neck. Yet her face is not frightening but happy, even blissful. What she presents is the joy of transcending the body, not the pain of losing it. She is also the most energetic form of the Goddess and shows the power of transformation in action.

Hence the severed head is not dead but in fact more alive. Consciousness is not limited to the body. It is a sphere of perception that dwells in the head but can function on its own apart from the body. Only when separated from body consciousness does awareness attain its real life and freedom, compared to which body consciousness has always been symbolized as a cage or tomb. In the body, consciousness is confined to the limited realm of the senses and their outward grasp. Liberated from the body, consciousness has the vision of infinity which includes the entire universe as itself.

While the idea of going beyond body consciousness can be frightening to us, the idea of remaining bound to body consciousness — and hence to time and death — should be more frightening. As it is, we are all trapped in the dense realm of physical matter, limited to the windows of the senses for whatever restricted and often misleading information we get. We only experience that portion of the infinite light of reality which can be refracted (and distorted) through the narrow openings of our senses. The pleasure that the body can bring us is much less than the pain, sorrow and disease. And we are condemned to repeated birth and death until we work our way out of the body cocoon.

From this state of entrapment in the limited sensitivity of the gross flesh, the Goddess Chhinnamasta appears as the great liberator and savioress. In her ecstasy as the Eternal she can drink all the blood, all the joys and sorrows of embodied life. She can absorb all the experiences of time, including disappointment and suffering, without forgetting her true nature. Though fierce in form she represents the most beneficent of energies.

PRACHANDA CHANDIKA

Chhinnamasta is called Prachanda Chandika or the fiercest form of Chandi (Kali). She is closely related to Kali but is the specific application of Kali's energy, directed toward the actual moment of transformation.

As a fierce Goddess she is related to Bhairavi and is similarly a warrioress. Yet while Bhairavi relates to the root energies of the Earth, Chhinnamasta relates to the dynamic forces of the Atmosphere. Chhinnamasta shows the combined manifest and unmanifest light in the intermediate world which mediates between the transcendent and the immanent, the lightning that unites Heaven and Earth (mind and body) in order to liberate us from their limitations.

While Chandi destroys the demons, Prachanda Chandi destroys the ultimate demon or negative entity, the ego. When this is destroyed, all negativity is forever eliminated.

INDRANI

Chhinnamasta is regarded as the same as Indrani, the consort of Indra, the supreme Lord in the *Vedas*, and hence she is the most important of the Vedic Goddesses. Indrani is called Vairochani, or the widely effulgent, and is thereby related to Durga, who is lauded by the same name. She is Vajra Vairochani, "she who is effulgent with the vajra or thunderbolt," which is the weapon of Indra, who himself is the vajra-being, the personification of instantaneous enlightenment.

LIGHTNING OR ELECTRICAL FORCE

As the power of Indra, Chhinnamasta is vidyut or lightning, the electrical energy of transformation (Vidyut Shakti) working in the cosmos on all levels. The electricity in the material world is only one form of this. In the mind it functions as the power of instantaneous enlightenment. While Kali rules over this force generally, Chhinnamasta represents the same force directed as the weapon of the Supreme for immediate transformation. She is the lightening bolt of insight which destroys the powers of the ignorance and lifts us beyond the skies.

As lightning, Chhinnamasta represents direct perception, pure seeing which cuts through everything and reveals the infinite beyond all forms. She is the power of self-vision which sacrifices all objects, including our own bodies, to the reality of pure awareness. She represents the Atma-yajna or Self-sacrifice, wherein we offer ourselves to the Divine through the sacrifice of the mind.

THE POWER OF DESTRUCTION

Chhinnamasta represents the pralaya or end of the world wherein the Absolute reabsorbs or swallows up all creation. She is the head that swallows up the entire body. Hence she is the power of destruction which is the negation of the manifest sphere into the unborn and uncreate beyond.

CHHINNAMASTA AND KUNDALINI

According to yogic science there are three knots (granthis) which prevent the movement of energy from flowing up the Sushumna of the subtle body. These are the Brahma-granthi in the Root Chakra which represents our bondage to speech, the Vishnu-granthi in the Heart Chakra showing our bondage to emotion, and the Rudra-granthi in the third eye showing our bondage to thought. Chhinnamasta represents the piercing of the Rudra-granthi or the knot in the head, allowing us to transcend thought, the mind and body consciousness altogether.

Chhinnamasta thus represents the free flow of energy through the Sushumna. She is the Kundalini Shakti flowing upward from the base of the spine to burst open the Crown Chakra and stream out into the infinite. She shows the energy of Kundalini awake and moving upwards toward transformation. She is Kundalini in her active and assertive role. As such, she represents the Vedic Path of the Gods (Devayana), which is the movement of the Prana up the Sushumna to the formless realms of pure consciousness, symbolized by the Sun.

The Sushumna is the central light of the subtle body. The other channels are its rays. If awareness is kept in the Sushumna, we move upward into the Divine. If our consciousness goes out through its rays or secondary channels, we move into the worlds of lesser experience, karma and rebirth. The key both to our spiritual growth and to avoiding negative karma is to keep our attention in the Sushumna. However, the Sushumna is the same as the Void, an objectless state. To stay in it requires dwelling in pure seeing. At death, the consciousness of practitioners of this Yoga goes up the Sushumna and exits by the top of the head. Those who don't know this Yoga exit by other channels and get lost in the subtle worlds.

Many yogis keep their consciousness in the Sushumna and don't try to open the chakras along its course. They direct their energy totally upward to break open the lid of the mind, and avoid the other chakras as a distraction. Meditating on Chhinnamasta we can raise the Kundalini directly from the Third Eye. Chhinnamasta is thus sacred to the Siddhas (yogic adepts) who have rent asunder the veil of the mind. The way to the realms (Lokas) of the Siddhas is through her. Those seeking to contact the Siddhas should worship her.

Yogini

Chhinnamasta is the great yogini (female yogi). She is the Yoga Shakti or power of Yoga in its most dramatic action. Hence she is known as Vajra Yogini. She is the Para-Dakini, the supreme or foremost of the Dakinis, the attendant Goddesses on the yogic path. As such she should be worshipped by those seeking yogic and occult powers.

LOCATION IN THE BODY

Chhinnamasta relates to the Third Eye (Ajña Chakra), which is her chief place of action. She represents the opened Third Eye from which comes the lightning of direct perception that destroys all duality and negativity. As the upward movement of the Prana she is associated with Udana Vayu, the upward moving of the vital airs, which the yogis seek to develop. Yet wherever there is seeing, there is her action. Her perceptive power can be taken to any center or chakra to perceive its nature and function.

MEDITATION FORM

Chhinnamasta has a naked headless body, and in her two hands holds her own severed head and a sword. With her severed head, via a long and stretched out tongue, she ecstatically drinks the central stream of blood which flows from her headless trunk. The severed head is located in her right hand, often portrayed as placed inside a skull cup. The sword or head-chopper is located in the left.

Her body is that of a girl of sixteen years of age and is adorned with a garland of severed heads and necklaces of bones. She wears a serpent as the sacred thread on her upper torso, and she has large breasts which are covered by lotus flowers. Her hair is spread out in strands like lightning and adorned with various flowers, with a single gem tied by a serpent as a cord at the top. Her three eyes are wide open and emanating light.

She has two companions called Dakini and Varnini to her left and right. She dances on the bodies of Kama, the God of love, and his consort Rati, who are in a sexual embrace. In some portrayals it is Radha and Krishna upon whom she dances. The form of Chhinnamasta is the same as the Vajra Yogini of the Buddhist Tantric tradition.

The central spurt of blood represents the flow of energy through the central channel or Sushumna. The right and left flows show the flows through the solar and lunar channels, the Pingala and Ida. Chhinnamasta, personifying the Sushumna, drinks the central stream. Varnini, personifying the Pingala, drinks the right stream. Dakini, personifying the Ida, drinks the left stream. The couple below her in a sexual embrace shows the inner union of the male and female energies in the psyche.

Her cut-off head is the liberated consciousness. Her hair like lightning and her eyes beaming light show her direct perception of the Absolute. Her sword or head-chopper is the power of discrimination (viveka). Her tongue is the power of mantra or the Divine Word. As her form is difficult to sculpt, it is rare to find except in drawings and paintings.

MANTRA

Chhinnamasta has an extended mantra of fifteen syllables. It is based on her name as Vajra Vairochani, the effulgent lightning bolt of direct perception. Its prime seed syllable is Hrīm.

Om śrīm hrīm hrīm aim vajra-vairocanīyai hūm hūm phaṭ svāhā!

Shrīm is a mantra of beauty and light. Hrīm is the mantra of inner transformation. Vajra-vairocaniyai means "to Vajra Vairocani," to the lightning of spiritual realization. Hūm gives the power to cut through illusions. Phaṭ serves to concentrate the force of the mantra. Svāhā offers it to the inner fire of Awareness.

Bhairava, the fierce form of Shiva, is the seer of her mantra as well as of Bhairavi's. Her mantra requires the terrible vision of the infinite (Bhairava), in which all finite things become nothing but dust or bubbles, to endure the power and the velocity of her illumining force. The Vedic deity Indra can also be worshipped as her lord. The Chhinnamasta Yantra can be used along with the mantra. She is also sometimes related to the mantra of wrath and fire, Hūm, as a single mantra.

MEDITATION APPROACHES

Chhinnamasta is perhaps the main form of the Goddess for those who practice the Yoga of knowledge (Jñana Yoga) as she represents the state of seeing. Many of the methods of the Yoga of knowledge relate to her worship, particularly meditation on the perceptual process itself, or the discrimination between the seer and the seen, whereby we withdraw the identification of our self-nature with all thoughts or objects. However, Chhinnamasta as Yogini aids us in all yogic practices, particularly those which require mastering the Kundalini.

To best worship Chhinnamasta, one should meditate upon the seer and withdraw one's attention from the objects seen. This is based upon the recognition that the seer is not an object, and that anything cognized by the mind as an object of perception, including the ego or self-image, must be apart from our true nature.

Another method is to merge one's mind into the state of seeing and forget both subject and object. This requires that we concentrate on the nature of seeing and stop dwelling on the seer or the seen. Hence the cultivation of pure and direct perception is the prime method of worshipping Chhinnamasta. This requires cultivating awareness and no longer trying to locate our reality in any time, place or person.

Actually we don't really see any objects. We merely have perceptions, which our thoughts, through the naming process, designate as various objects. If we cease to identify our perceptions as objects via thought, we do not find anything apart from consciousness. The world is like a kaleidoscopic pattern of perceptions which our thoughts divide up into various objects, but apart from the division of thought have no other substantiality.

Perception is not separate from the seer. If we cease to focus on perception as real, and introvert our consciousness into the seer, the kaleidoscopic pattern of perception will resolve itself like waves into the ocean of pure awareness.

GANAPATI MUNI

Prachanda Chandi's modern seer is Ganapati Muni, who experienced in his own life the breaking open of the skull. After this event a column of light or vapor could be observed coming from his head, which his disciples and other yogis noticed.

DHUMAVATI YANTRA

7
DHUMAVATI:
The Grandmother Spirit

Perceived as the Void, as the dissolved form of consciousness, when all beings are dissolved in sleep in the supreme Brahman, having swallowed the entire universe, the seer-poets call her the most glorious and the eldest, Dhumavati.

She exists in the forms of sleep, lack of memory, illusion, and dullness in the creatures immersed in the illusion of the world, but among the yogis she becomes the power that destroys all thoughts, indeed Samadhi itself.
— Ganapati Muni, Uma Sahasram 38. 13–14

THE GRANDMOTHER SPIRIT

Dhumavati is the eldest among the Goddesses, the Grandmother Spirit. She stands behind the other Goddesses as their ancestral guide. As the Grandmother Spirit she is the great teacher who bestows the ultimate lessons of birth and death. She is the knowledge that comes through hard experience, in which our immature and youthful desires and fantasies are put to rest.

Dhuma means "smoke." Dhumavati is "one who is composed of smoke." Her nature is not illumination but obscuration. However, to obscure one thing is to reveal another. By obscuring or covering all that is known, Dhumavati reveals the depth of the unknown and the unmanifest. Dhumavati obscures what is evident in order to reveal the hidden and the profound.

Dhumavati is portrayed as a widow. She is the feminine principle devoid of the masculine principle. She is Shakti without Shiva as a pure potential energy without any will to motivate it. Thus she contains within herself all potentials and shows the latent energies that dwell within us. To develop these latent energies we must first recognize them. This requires honoring Dhumavati.

Dhumavati shows the feminine principle of negation in all of its aspects. On an outer level she represents poverty, destitution, and suffering, the great misfortunes that we all fear in life. Hence she is said to be

DHUMAVATI

crooked, troublesome, and quarrelsome — a witch or a hag. Yet on an inner level this same negativity causes us to seek a greater fulfillment than can be achieved in the limited realms of the manifest creation. After all, only frustration in our outer life causes us to seek the inner reality. Dhumavati is whatever obstructs us in life, but what obstructs us in one area can release a new potential to grow in a different direction. Thus she is the good fortune that comes to us in the form of misfortune.

PRIMORDIAL DARKNESS

Dhumavati represents the darkness on the face of the deep, the original chaos and obscurity which underlies creation. She is the darkness of primordial ignorance, Mulavidya, from which this world of illusion has arisen, and which it is seeking to transcend. The truth is that we are born in ignorance. It is not some theory but the hard and clear fact of our existence. We don't really know who we are or where we are going in life. Our life is a limited light between two greater darknesses. Hence Dhumavati or smoke embraces us on both sides.

Dhumavati represents the power of ignorance or that aspect of the creative force which causes the obscuration of the underlying light of consciousness. While Maya is the magic or illusion power of the Lord that makes the one reality appear as many, ignorance is a form of darkness which prevents us from seeing the underlying reality.

Yet ignorance has a higher meaning. Only when we recognize that we are ignorant, that we really don't know anything, can we begin to learn. Moreover, as we grow in consciousness we recognize that the ordinary mind has no real capacity for true knowledge, that true knowledge only begins when we set the ordinary thought process aside. It is not so much that we do not know as that what we call knowledge can never take us to the truth. For yogis this higher ignorance means ignoring or forgetting the movements of the mind, letting go of all fears, desires, likes and dislikes, opinions and beliefs. By no longer recognizing any reality outside of consciousness we go beyond the field of death.

Dhumavati is thus the primal sleep wherein all the creatures of the universe are dissolved in the underlying reality of the Supreme Brahman. She is also Yoga-nidra or the yogic sleep in which the yogi is merged into the pre-creation state of consciousness and no longer perceives the external world. She represents the bliss of the before-creation state, wherein the formless Brahman alone exists. She helps us to forget the bad dream of Samsara and return to the blissful being of Nirvana. She is the wisdom of forgetting.

THE VOID

Dhumavati is the void, wherein all forms have been dissolved and nothing can any longer be differentiated. Yet this void is not mere darkness. It is a self-illumining reality free of the ordinary duality of subject and object. Hence Vedanta states that the Goddess appears as the Void but is not really void, as even the void can only exist relative to the Seer. In fact the true void or immaterial state is consciousness itself. As such, Dhumavati is pure, perfect and full Awareness in which there are no longer any objects. The Void is not merely emptiness but the cessation of the movements of the mind. Dhumavati is thus ultimately silence itself.

THE POWER OF SUFFERING

Dhumavati represents the negative powers of life: disappointment, frustration, humiliation, defeat, loss, sorrow and loneliness. Such experiences overpower the ordinary mind, but to the yogi they are special doors of opportunity to contact the reality which transcends desire. To recognize in these negative experiences of life the great Grandmother Goddess and her lessons is to gain a great victory for the soul. For such brave souls Dhumavati grants the virtues of patience, perseverance, forgiveness and detachment. She turns her devotees into great teachers for humanity.

Dhumavati reveals the imperfect, transient, unhappy and confused state of ordinary egoic existence in order that we may transcend it. Her form is not pleasant but shows the dark shadow of the world so that we may no longer be entranced by its superficial joys. Honoring these "negative" experiences as the wisdom of the ancient Goddess helps us transmute them into energies of delight.

DHUMAVATI AND KALI

Dhumavati is the elder form of Kali, Kali as an old woman. She represents time or the life-force dissociated from the process of manifestation. She is the timeless which never really enters into the process of time. She is not revealed in the ordinary world but present as a background screen or smoke that helps us see beyond the evident forms around us. Those who are trying to ward off negative influences should worship Dhumavati. She gives transcendence and freedom, returning us to the condition prior to the arising of any negative forces.

LOCATION IN THE BODY

Dhumavati is another Goddess that relates to the heart or the middle region. But her energy is withdrawn, either apart from manifestation, or recoiling from it. Hence she is only vaguely present anywhere, though her spirit looms behind everything.

MEDITATION FORM

Dhumavati is portrayed as a tall and thin old woman with disheveled and matted hair. She is fearful, unattractive and dark in complexion, with a wrinkled face, and her limbs are red. She has a harsh look in her eyes and she is missing a number of her teeth, which are otherwise large in size. Sometimes she is portrayed with fangs and her nose is long and snout-like. She is dressed in old or dirty clothes and her breasts hang down. She rides a chariot whose insignia is a crow. In her left hand she carries a winnowing basket and with her right makes the gesture of knowledge (cinmudra). In other accounts she carries a skull-cup and sword in her two hands. She wears a garland of severed heads and is ever hungry and thirsty, always provoking quarrels and misunderstandings.

The winnowing basket shows the need to discern the inner essence from the illusory reality of outer forms. Her fearful appearance is intended not to frighten us but to reveal the danger of considering sensory pleasure as bringing fulfillment. As the ugly form of the Goddess she teaches us to look beyond apparent beauty to the inner truth. We could say that this is the image of the witch. Yet the witch in yogic circles is not just a negative spirit. Teaching us the negative side of life, she liberates us from attachment and unfolds the inner realities.

MANTRA

Dhumavati's mantra is essentially the same as her seed-syllable Dhūm repeated.

Dhūm dhūm dhūmāvati svāhā!

Dhūm means "smoke" or "to obscure." This mantra obscures or darkens all false lights. It creates a protective smoke that hides us from any negativity. Ultimately it negates our apparent existence so that the God of death cannot find us.

The seer of the mantra is Pippalada, a famous sage of the *Atharva Veda* and *Prashna Upanishad*, known for his special knowledge of Prana. Yet technically Dhumavati has no Shiva or masculine form with which the seer of her mantra can be identified. The Dhumavati Yantra can be used along with her mantra.

MEDITATION APPROACHES

Dhumavati's worship consists in discarding all thought waves and merging into the great unknown silence beyond. We begin to see her when we stop focusing on the outer forms of things and recognize the background presence in which they occur. This requires unfocusing our perception, no longer seeing the evident lines in things but noticing the background space instead. This requires giving up the false light of names and opinions and looking at all objects and events without any preconceptions, likes or dislikes.

Meditation upon the Void as the supreme reality, on non-being as the ultimate source and end of all manifest beings, is another method of relating to her. Meditation upon impermanence or the transient nature of all things is yet another approach.

We contact Dhumavati when we withdraw from the known, stop seeking anything in the realm of time, become totally disillusioned and detached from all apparent realities, and learn to rest in our unborn nature. Giving reverence to sorrow and disappointment as Divine friends who have come to teach us the limitations of the body-mind is another means of honoring her wisdom.

BAGALAMUKHI YANTRA

8

BAGALAMUKHI:
The Hypnotic Power of the Goddess

*Oh Mother, the power of stopping all things in the
microcosm and the macrocosm, is your single great power
as Bagala.* — *Ganapati Muni, Uma Sahasram 38.17*

Beauty can have a stunning effect upon us. A very beautiful woman
walking by can make a man stop and lose his breath. Beauty can cause us
to lose our senses and become dumbstruck. The cosmic feminine power
has a capacity to stun, stop or paralyze. These are aspects of the Goddess
Bagalamukhi, who represents the hypnotic power of the Goddess. Bagala
means literally a "rope" or a "bridle;" Mukhi means "face." Bagalamukhi
is one whose face has the power to control or conquer. Bagalamukhi is
often called simply Bagala.

THE POWER OF SILENCE
Bagala is a Goddess of speech, and as such is related to Tara and
regarded as a form of her. When sound becomes manifest as light, Tara
becomes Bagala. When the brilliant light of speech comes forth, then Tara
gains the effulgence of Bagala and causes all things to become still. Bagala
is thus the stunning radiance that comes forth from the Divine Word and
puts the human or egoistic word to rest.

Bagala gives a power of speech that leaves others silent and grasping
for words. She gives the decisive statement, the irrefutable conclusion,
the pronouncement of ultimate truth. Hence she is propitiated for success
in discussions and debates. No one can defeat her because she has the truth
power of the Self-nature.

THE WEAPON OF BRAHMAN
The weapon that puts an end to all conflict and confusion is the
weapon of spiritual knowledge, the weapon of Brahman (Brahmastra).
The highest form of the Brahmastra is the question "Who am I?" or "What
is the Self?"

If we look deeply we see that, though we may know external things,
our Self remains unknown to us. What we call our self is merely some

BAGALAMUKHI

temporary thought, emotion, or sensation with which we are identified, but not the nature of our consciousness itself. If we continually bring the mind back to this question, Who am I? it will put an end to all our wandering thoughts and make all other questions and seekings appear unimportant. This is how Tara or Om, the Divine Word, becomes a force of inquiry to bring us to stillness or the power of Bagala. Om itself is the mantra of the Divine I Am, which causes us to ask who we are. What is our Self-nature? What is the I Am in itself once divested of all transient identifications with which we confuse it? Such questions will bring the mind to rest.

The Commander of the Divine Army

Bagala gives us the power to overcome hostile forces, which inwardly are the negative thoughts and emotions born of the ego. She is speech used as a weapon to destroy negativity. She is similar to Bhairavi but whereas Bhairavi burns away all opposition, Bagala crushes and dissolves it, freezes it as it were. Negativity is not so much a force that has to be destroyed as a distracted state of mind that must be brought to rest.

Bagala is similar to Chinnamasta, as both have an electrical, lightning, or vajra-force. However, whereas Chinnamasta gives the power to see through things, which proceeds through perception, Bagala gives the power to stop them, which proceeds through the Word. Both Goddesses should be worshipped by those seeking radical changes in their lives and their view of reality. As Chinnamasta cuts through illusion, Bagalamukhi smashes the false constructions of the mind.

Bagala is commander of the army for the Supreme Goddess and represents her striking force. While Chinnamasta is able to freeze or stop our perception, Bagala has the same effect upon our speech, thought, and Pranic activity. She represents the central point of stillness behind all activity, through which all action is mastered. Bagala commands the danda (staff or rod) whereby Divine justice is meted out for wrong actions. She also represents the one-pointedness or power of attention that ends all confusion.

Stambhana

Many yogic and magical practices aim at developing the power of stambhana, which literally means "stopping" or "paralyzing." On an outer level it is the power to stop or paralyze those who would attack us, particularly to destroy their power of speech, which being eliminated, renders a person impotent. It is also the power to hypnotise others and get them to act according to our will. On an inner level it is the mastery of our own thoughts and energies.

Bagala grants complete control over our movements and the capacity to stop them at will. Such stopping comes from and promotes self-awareness. It develops detachment as it prevents us from becoming identified with what we do. To promote this awareness, we must learn to stop and observe ourselves during ordinary daily activities. We can literally stop ourselves in midmotion to observe our state of mind when we are busy, engaged or disturbed. Or we can continue with our actions but keep our mind in the quiescent state of the observer.

The truth is that we have forgotten ourselves and are hypnotized by the allure of external objects and identities. Bagala breaks this external hypnosis through the greater hypnotic power of spiritual knowledge that causes us to lose interest in the idea of an external reality.

THE REVERSAL OF OPPOSITES

Bagala turns each thing into its opposite. She turns speech into silence, knowledge into ignorance, power into impotence, defeat into victory. She represents the knowledge whereby each thing must in time become its opposite. As the still point between dualities she allows us to master them. We contact her grace when we see the opposite hidden in each situation and are no longer deceived by appearances. To see the failure hidden in success, the death hidden in life, or the joy hidden in sorrow are ways of contacting her reality. Bagala is the secret presence of the opposite wherein each thing is dissolved back into the Unborn and the Uncreate.

LOCATION WITHIN THE BODY

Bagala relates to the soft palate, the place called Indra-yoni, which is the middle point between the senses of the eyes, ears, nose and tongue. The soft palate is related in function with the third eye, and so Bagala, like Chinnamasta is associated with this chakra. Concentration on the point of the soft palate gives control over the senses and vital energies (Pranas).

Bagala also relates to the Heart Center as the prime site of Prana. Withdrawing all life-energies into the heart brings them to rest and gives us complete control over our entire existence, taking us beyond the fluctuations of life and death.

MEDITATION FORM

Bagala is another of the frightening forms of the Goddess. Her color is yellow. She is clad in yellow clothing and is adorned with yellow ornaments and yellow flowers (particularly the champak flower). With her left hand she catches hold of her opponent's tongue and with her right hand she strikes him on the head with her mace. She sits upon a golden throne surrounded by red lotuses. By some accounts she wears the crescent moon as a jewel on her head.

Her yellow color (which generally is made with turmeric root) shows her bright and cleansing energy. Yellow shows the radiance of knowledge that overcomes all darkness. For her worship one should also dress in yellow. Her opponent is the ego. She pulls out the tongue of the ego, which is the attachment to gossip, opinions, and all negative speech patterns that are the essence of the self-focused mind. As long as we are involved in such negative speech patterns we must come to experience the wrath of Bagala.

MANTRA

The prime mantra for Bagalamukhi the seed-syllable Hlrīm. The addition of the la-sound to the mantra Hrīm gives it the power to stop things. She also has an extended mantra.

Om hlrīm bagalāmukhi sarvaduṣṭānām vācam mukham padam stambhaya jihvām kīlaya buddhim vināśaya hlrīm om svāhā!

The mantra means "Bagalāmukhi, paralyze (stambhaya) the place of speech (vacham padam) in the mouth (mukham) of all those who would harm us (saravduṣtanam), suppress their tongue (jihvām kīlaya), destroy their minds (buddhim vināśaya)." However, whatever we think of as being other than ourselves defeats us, as the *Upanishads* proclaim. The ultimate enemy to be paralyzed is the ego and its duality of self and other, which divides the energy of our own awareness. The negative power of the ego manifests mainly through wrong speech. This must be stopped for thought to be controlled and for meditation to develop. The key to controlling thought is to first control our speech. This can be done through the mantra to Bagala. The Bagalamukhi Yantra can be used along with the mantra.

YOGIC APPROACHES:
BAGALAMUKHI AS THE GODDESS OF YOGA

As there are many forms of Stambhana or stopping action, there are many ways to worship this Goddess, who herself is symbolic of the entire process of Yoga aiming at silencing the mind. The most basic practice is to control speech by not saying anything harmful to other creatures.

The practice of Hatha Yoga relates to her way of knowledge, particularly asana (yogic postures), wherein a specific posture is maintained without any movement. A deeper way to worship her is to arrest the movement of the Prana or life-force through Pranayama. However, one cannot simply and forcefully try to stop the breath. Only the Goddess power (Yoga Shakti) can do this. Hence her grace must be sought first.

Another way to worship this Goddess is to learn to stop our energy at will, through mere thought or mantra. This requires Raja Yoga. One such method is to develop concentration (dharana) and become able to fix our attention at will upon any object. The highest object of attention is our own Self, which we should concentrate on in the third eye or in the heart. The cultivation of the will is important to the worship of Bagala. For this we should have the will to know the truth and put it into action.

Yet another method is to continually try to remember our true nature. This fixes our attention and removes us from external seeking. It is like trying to remember something special that one has forgotten. Watch the movement of the mind in this process, how steady it becomes. Steady remembrance of the Self is the best way to worship Bagala. The yogic negation of all thought relates to her.

However, her worship need not be described in only a negative way. It arises through the power of observation, whereby we look upon things from the standpoint of the witness or observer. Once we are no longer identified with the movements of the mind, we gain control over them and can stop them at will.

There is a flow of the energy of consciousness up the Sushumna from the heart to the Crown Chakra. There it cools and flows down as a cool current through the channels of the subtle body. If one stops or blocks the upward flow at the Third Eye, it results in inherence in the Self. Remaining there gives Self-awareness in the waking state. If the current is stopped in the region of the soft palate, it gives Self-awareness in the dream state. If the flow is arrested at its source in the heart, it gives Self-awareness in the deep sleep state.

MATANGI YANTRA

9
MATANGI:
The Utterance of the Divine Word

Dark emerald Mother, Matangi, abounding in joy,
auspicious let your side-glance fall on us, you who dwell
in the forest of bliss.
Victory to the daughter of the sage Matanga, who has
the color of a dark blue lotus, victory to the nectar of all
song, victory to her who loves the playful parrot.
— Shyamaladandakam 3–4

MATANGI AS THE SPOKEN WORD

Mata literally means "a thought" or "an opinion." Matangi is thus the Goddess power which has entered into thought or the mind. She is the word as the embodiment of thought. She also relates to the ear and our ability to listen, which is the origin of true understanding that forms powerful thoughts. Matangi bestows knowledge, talent and expertise. She is the Goddess of the spoken word and of any outward articulation of inner knowledge, including all forms of art, music and dance.

Matangi is the last of the three Goddesses who relate to the Divine Word, the other two being Tara and Bhairavi. Like Tara she is a Goddess of learning and eloquence. However, whereas Tara represents the illumined word (Pashyanti), Matangi represents the spoken word (Vaikhari), while Bhairavi is the Goddess of the transcendent and unmanifest form of speech (Para). Yet Matangi can also represent the middle form of speech (Madhyama), which governs the ideas that we are putting into words and thereby our thinking process. In her highest role, Matangi represents Para-Vaikhari or the supreme Word as manifest through audible speech, which is the direct revelation of the highest knowledge in human speech from which all true scripture arises. As such Matangi encompasses all levels of speech.

MATANGI AND SARASVATI

Matangi relates to Sarasvati, the Goddess of wisdom and the consort of Lord Brahma, the creator of the universe. Matangi, like Sarasvati, plays a vina and rules over music or audible sound in general, not just the spoken

MATANGI

word. She is the manifest form of song. Like Sarasvati she is symbolized by the rain cloud and by the thunder, as well as by the rivers pouring into the sea. She is the vibratory sound, Nada, that flows in the subtle channels, Nadis, down through our entire body and mind.

However, Matangi and Sarasvati are a little different. Matangi is the form of Sarasvati directed towards inner knowledge. She is her dark, mystic, ecstatic or wild form. Sarasvati is often a Goddess of only ordinary learning, art and culture. Matangi rules over the extraordinary, which takes us beyond the bounds of the conventional. Matangi is an outcast or artist who goes against the norms of society, while Sarasvati represents the knowledge and virtue of the Brahmin or learned class which never departs from propriety. Matangi is that portion of Sarasvati which is allied with the transforming energy of Kali.

MATANGI AS THE GURU

The guru (spiritual teacher) instructs us through the spoken word. Hence his vehicle among the Goddesses is Matangi. Matangi represents the teachings of the guru and the tradition. She represents the continuity of spiritual instruction in the world. By honoring her we also honor the guru. Those seeking to teach others, particularly to communicate to the masses of people, should seek the grace of Matangi.

MATANGI AND GANESHA

Mata also means "wild" or "passionate." Matangi is one who is wild or passionate in limbs or movement. Matangi also means a female elephant. In Hindu mythology the elephant relates to Ganesha, the first son of Shiva and Parvati, who was fitted with the head of an elephant. Ganesha is similarly the Lord of the Word and the Lord of knowledge as well as the remover of all obstacles. Hence mantras to him precede any teaching process, like the chanting of the *Vedas*, as well as the ordinary activities of life like marriage, travel, and business ventures.

Matangi is related to Ganesha and, on one level, is his consort. Generally the two consorts of Ganesha are called Buddhi, intelligence, and Siddhi, accomplishment. These same powers are represented by Matangi. Like Ganesha she can be propitiated to remove obstacles and give accomplishments, as well as to grant knowledge.

MATANGI AS THE OUTCAST

Matangi is described as an outcast and as impure. On one level, this refers to the nature of the spoken word, which is inherently limited in what it can project. Only if we look to the Goddess power, Matangi, behind the

the screen of words, will we be free from the impurity inherent in trying to put anything into words. The word makes things profane. Naming often causes us to misapprehend and devalue the thing itself. Numbers, titles, descriptions, and explanations become barriers to our actual contact with the soul in things. Matangi rules over these articulations of language and gives the power to use them the right way and to go beyond them.

However, there is another level on which Matangi is the outcast or the residue. The Self or Atman transcends the laws of nature and is beyond good and evil. Matangi as the manifest knowledge of the Self takes us beyond such outward limitations and conventions and makes us outcasts, transcending the human world altogether. Self-realized being sometimes appear poor, crazy or in some way unusual. This is another part of Matangi, who is the visible appearance of the highest knowledge. Matangi is the highest of the Goddesses in that she allows all their powers and principles to be realized.

According to the *Upanishads* the essence of the human being is speech. What we express through speech is the final product of all that we take into ourselves in life. This ultimate residue and representation of who we are through speech is Matangi. This, however, is not ordinary or casual speech, but the deepest expression of our hearts.

MATANGI AND JOY

The Divine Word has power, feeling, and passion, which is not mere human emotion but Divine bliss. The Divine Word is not merely a theoretical or practical statement but an effusion of energy and delight. This joy is another aspect of Matangi. Matangi is thus a wild, playful and ecstatic Goddess.

Matangi as the manifest creative word represents the great powers of nature, wherein the Divine Word is embodied. She personifies all the beauty, passion and power of the tropical jungle or rain forest, where she happily dwells like a mad elephant, reflecting the primal rhythms of Mother Nature. In this regard her forms are sometimes mixed with those of Sundari. She is similarly the beauty of all creation in the Self, but whereas for Sundari the inner experience of consciousness is predominant, for Matangi the outer expression gains prominence.

MATANGI AS THE MINISTER

Matangi represents the ministerial power of the Goddess. She is the counselor to Rajarajeshvari or Tripura Sundari, the Supreme Queen of the universe. As such she is called Mantrini and has power over all mantras, particularly in their vocalization and articulation. She gives us the ability to communicate with all the other Gods and Goddesses through the power of the mantra. In fact she rules over all forms of knowledge, counseling and teaching. Those seeking proficiency in these areas should honor Matangi.

LOCATION IN THE BODY

Matangi resides in the Throat Chakra, the center of speech. She also resides on the tip of the tongue, the place wherein speech is articulated and wherein we are able to taste the essences of things.

There is a special nerve or channel of the subtle body called Sarasvati that runs from the Third Eye to the tip of the tongue, which relates to her. This is the stream of inspiration from the mind to its expression via speech. Matangi represents the flow of bliss through this channel, which makes us poet-seers of the Divine with all the powers of cosmic creativity.

MEDITATION FORM

Matangi's meditation form is as follows:

> *Playing a ruby-studded vina, ecstatic, delighting in sweet speech, I remember the daughter of the sage Matanga, who has soft dark-emerald limbs.*
>
> *Who has four arms, and wears the crescent moon for an ornament, with uprisen breasts, anointed with the red kumkum powder, who carries a sugar-cane bow, a noose, a hook, and flower arrows in her hand, I honor you, the One Mother of the universe.* — *Shyamaladandakam 1–2*

Matangi is dark emerald green in color, the color of deep knowledge and profound life-energy, which is also the color of the planet Mercury that governs intelligence. She plays the vina, a stringed instrument like a sitar, which shows her musical and vibratory power. She is beautiful and carries various weapons with which to fascinate and subdue us. In this regard she has the same ornaments and weapons as Sundari. She is often said to have a parrot in her hands, which represents the powers of speech as inherent in nature. She sits on a throne made of gems.

MANTRA

Matangi can be worshipped by the mantra Aim, which is the mantra sacred to Sarasvati and is the seed-syllable of wisdom, learning, teaching and hence the very voice of the guru or inner guide. Matangi herself possesses a longer mantra of twenty syllables, which includes Aim.

Om hrīm aim śrīm namo bhagavati ucchiṣṭacāṇḍāli
śrī matāṅgeśvari sarvajanavaśankari svāhā!

The mantra begins with Om hrīm aim śrīm, Om being the infinite, Hrīm transformation, Aim knowledge, and Shrīm glory. The mantra itself means "Reverence to Adorable Matangi, the outcast and residue, who gives control over all creatures." As the residue she is the Divine Self that is left over when all things perish. Through her mantric force she gives us the power over all creatures, who by her delight become our friends and companions. The Matangi Yantra can be used along with the mantra.

MEDITATION APPROACHES

The main worship of Matangi is to recite the teachings, particularly great scriptures, like the *Vedas*, which embody the power of sound. The power of the mantra is connected with its sound. This power cannot be received through mere translations and their recitation. Such chants should be done in their original language.

Chanting of the Sanskrit alphabet is one of the best ways to worship Matangi. The letters of the alphabet represent unmanifest sound, as opposed to the manifest differentiation of sound as various words. Chanting the Sanskrit alphabet can be allied with the petals of the chakras and used to help open them. Such chanting begins with the vowels corresponding to the Throat Chakra and continues through the alphabet down to the Root Chakra. In other words, it begins with Matangi.

Another way to worship Matangi is to reflect upon the meaning of the teachings, particularly the word of the guru. This requires contemplation of the teachings and seeing how they relate to our own life and experience. Mantra has much more power if we understand it not merely intellectually but according to the cosmic principles by which it vibrates.

Music and song are other aspects of the worship of Matangi. She is specifically a Goddess of musicians. Yoga paths emphasizing music or the sound current, like Nada Yoga, relate to her. Meditation upon Matangi gives all powers of art and artistic expression.

Yet in her highest role we must recognize Matangi in her transcendent meaning as the silence of the Self-nature, which is the real essence and power behind all words and thoughts. Matangi is speech and art energized toward transcendence, to make the visible world, Samsara, a realm of Nirvana.

KAMALATMIKA YANTRA

10
KAMALATMIKA:
The Lotus Goddess of Delight

We adore Lakshmi, who has the nature of supreme peace and the lustre of pure gold, whose form is radiant, wearing gold and possessing all ornaments.

Who carries a golden chalice and a golden lotus, whose hands give gold, the original power, the Mother of all, who dwells at the side of Lord Vishnu.

— *Lakshmi Dhyanam*

THE GODDESS OF THE LOTUS

The lotus is the most sacred flower of the Hindus and of the people of east Asia in general. The lotus is a symbol of unfoldment: it represents the opening of the lotuses of the different chakras of the subtle body, particularly the lotus of the heart. Though the lotus puts its roots into the mud and grows in marshlands, it produces the most beautiful flower, like the soul coming forth from the earth of the physical body. The lotus is also a plant of great energy and its seeds give much vigor when taken as a food.

Kamalatmika is one whose nature is of the lotus. She is sometimes just called Kamala, which is one of the many Sanskrit names for lotus. The lotus Goddess is Lakshmi, the consort of Lord Vishnu, the preserver of the universe. Lakshmi arises out of a lotus from the cosmic ocean. Kamala is Lakshmi among the Ten Wisdom Goddesses. Lakshmi is the Goddess of wealth, beauty, fertility, love, and devotion, like Roman Venus and Greek Aphrodite, who, like Lakshmi, is born from the ocean, but on a sea shell rather than a lotus. Lakshmi is the great Mother in her role of fulfilling all desires. She represents the water of fulfillment, the flowering of Divine grace and love.

KAMALA AND SUNDARI

Kamala is similar to Sundari in that both rule over love, beauty and bliss. Sundari, however, rules over the subtle form of bliss born of perception of the Self. Kamala governs the outer form of beauty, not merely as pleasure but as the unfolding of the Divine nature into the realms

KAMALATMIKA

of action and creation. Kamala causes us to create forms in the outer world, while Sundari allows us to withdraw the outer world into our own consciousness. Kamala thus relates to the Earth, which contains the maximum manifestation of the Divine in the material word. The Earth Goddess, Bhu Devi, is considered to be the second consort of Lord Vishnu.

However, the special abode of Kamala is Heaven, the realm of celestial delight, wherein alone all desires can be fulfilled. In Heaven exists the celestial form of the Goddess as the essence of all the tanmatras (subtle sensory qualities), in which all wishes can be granted. This is the higher form of Kamala.

Kamala nourishes and supports whatever we truly aspire to do. She aids in all projects and ever seeks to promote their fulfillment, allowing layer upon layer of Divine grace to come forth in various degrees of wonder. She can be propitiated both for ordinary worldly goals and for spiritual realization. But the ordinary goals we seek through her — wealth, progeny, or success — should be part of seeking Divine fulfillment in life, an unfoldment of our soul's desires through an organic process of evolution, not a mere satisfying of neurotic wants.

MATERIAL AND SPIRITUAL WEALTH

Kamala is the form of the Goddess most worshipped by people in this world, as we are mainly cognizant of outer beauty and abundance. Most of us are engaged in the pursuit of pleasure, fortune, talent, fame and so on, which are nothing but superficial or limited aspects of the power of Lakshmi. Since we naturally pursue Lakshmi, we might as well pursue her highest form. The most beautiful thing in life is devotion to the Divine. Lakshmi also gives this. When we have that spirit of devotion for the Divine presence everywhere we find incomparable beauty and wealth in everything.

True richness, moreover, is not what we own but what we are able to give. Kamala symbolizes this spirit of giving that dispenses all that we might outwardly or inwardly seek. Yet we should be careful in what we seek, because it will eventually be given to us. Lakshmi or the fortune we seek leads to Kamala or its unfoldment. Hence if we are going to seek anything, we should seek everything. We should ask for nothing less than the Divine, an infinite, eternal and perfect existence, consciousness, and bliss (Sacchidananda). We should seek the total unfoldment of ourselves and of the universe and not merely content ourselves with transient goals. This is the real worship of Kamala or Lakshmi which puts an end to all outer seeking.

Kamala also relates to the beauty of perception whereby we see the Divine quality in each thing. The quality of our consciousness is our greatest wealth, not what we possess outwardly, which we can never really hold onto anyway. Part of the worship of Kamala is to unfold the full powers of inner perception in order to see the extraordinary beauty in the simple presence of nature and the Earth.

KAMALA, LAKSHMI AND KALI

Kamala is a little different from Lakshmi. Kamala is the aspect of Lakshmi that is part of the Wisdom Goddesses. She is the form of Lakshmi which relates specifically to the practice of Yoga. Hence she is also a form of Kali. Kali or the beauty of the void is also the basis of Kamala or the beauty of life. The spiritual lotus, which is the basis of the universal energy, blooms in the void. It comes forth in the space of pure consciousness. Hence to allow it to come forth we must first make ourselves empty and clear. Only the non-attachment of Kali enables us to enjoy life and find our fulfillment through Kamala.

Though Kamala is beneficent in form, she may appear as Kali and remove our head if we become attached to her delights. On the other hand, if we recognize Kali and surrender our desires to the eternal reality, then Kali appears as the beautiful and beneficent Kamala, granting us all good things in the glory of God.

THE LAST OF THE TEN WISDOM GODDESSES

Kamala as the tenth and last of the Wisdom Goddesses shows the full unfoldment of the power of the Goddess into the material sphere. Kamala is the beginning and the end of our worship of the Goddess. We first approach the Divine seeking help in achieving ordinary human wishes, like health, prosperity, and a happy family. We complete our understanding of the Divine by seeing its presence even in the ordinary things of human life, in the forms of nature and the Earth, discerning a Divine urge toward union hidden even in worldly desires.

LOCATION IN THE BODY

Kamala is located in the heart, specifically the Heart Chakra of the subtle body, which is the place of devotional worship. She is the image of the heart's delight and the heart's wish for perfect beauty and happiness. We should visualize this perfect fulfillment as the Divine grace that naturally comes to the hearts of all beings.

MEDITATION FORM

Kamala is golden in color, seated on a lotus, and with two of her hands she gives the gestures which grant boons and dispel fear. With her other two hands she carries lotuses, or sometimes one hand dispenses gold coins and the other carries a water pot. She is often portrayed with a lotus above her on either side and sitting with one leg hanging down. As Lakshmi she can be portrayed as being bathed by water from the trunks of elephants on each side.

The lotus is the symbol of inner unfoldment. Water is a symbol of spiritual grace, love and communion. Gold is the richness of perception and devotion. Kamala is abundance in all of its forms.

The Buddhist form of the Goddess Tara is generally portrayed in the same manner as Hindu Lakshmi, but with slightly different hand gestures. These two Goddesses are related as ruling over beauty, fertility and love. Tara in Hindu iconography also carries a lotus in one of her hands.

MANTRA

Kamala's seed-syllable (bija mantra) is the same as that of Lakshmi, Shrīm. Shrīm is the great mantra of beauty, abundance, splendor, devotion, surrender, and refuge. Like Lakshmi it grants all the goals of life up to the highest liberation. Hence it is one of the most important, auspicious and generally useful of all bija-mantras.

The seer of her mantra is the Rishi Bhrigu, one of the great repositories of spiritual and occult knowledge, identified with the planet Venus. Lakshmi is the daughter of Bhrigu, who is connected with the ocean and the ocean-God Varuna who is his father. Bhrigu along with Angiras, who is a form of Agni or fire, are the two main founders of the families of Vedic Rishis to whom most Hindus claim their descent. Bhrigu relates to Vishnu, while Angiras is Shiva. The Kamala Yantra or Lakshmi Yantra can be used along with the mantra for Kamala.

MEDITATION APPROACHES

One gives reverence to Kamala by recognizing the Divine beauty manifest in the world of nature. To do this one should meditate upon the rays of the Sun, not as material forces but as powers of Divine light, life and love which nourish all things and cause them to grow not only physically but with intelligence and virtue. The rays of the Sun, as shown in ancient Egyptian art and in the verses of the *Rig Veda*, are the hands of the Sun God (or Sun Goddess), whereby we are touched by Divine grace and enlightenment. Seeing the spiritual power of the solar radiance sets in motion the process of inner unfoldment which is Kamala.

Any acknowledgment of the Divine presence in outer forms of beauty and splendor is a worship of Kamala. This may be the appreciation of art or music, a beautiful sunset, a beautiful face, or just the joy of being alive. It also occurs when we ourselves participate in any spiritually creative work. More specifically the worship of Kamala involves putting an icon of the Goddess in our own home and doing daily worship and meditation on it.

All forms of devotional worship are aspects of Kamala. Most specifically puja — offering flowers, scents, incense, lights, and food to an image of the Goddess — is an important way to honor Kamala. But this should be done with knowledge, recognizing that the outer form is nothing but a reflection of the Goddess power that resides within our hearts.

11
RELATIONSHIPS
BETWEEN THE WISDOM GODDESES

As they constitute a complete system of knowledge, there are a number of ways to correlate the Ten Wisdom Goddesses. Generally they fall into two groups of five. The first five represent the prime principles of existence.

Kali	Time
Tara	Word
Sundari	Light
Bhuvanesvari	Space
Bhairavi	Energy

The next five represent the main methods of transformation in the practice of Yoga.

Chhinnamasta	Perception
Dhumavati	Voidness
Bagalamukhi	Stillness
Matangi	Knowledge
Kamala	Delight

These two groups go together:

Kali-Chhinnamasta	Time and transformation
Tara-Matangi	Word, unmanifest and manifest
Sundari-Kamala	Beauty, unmanifest and manifest
Bhuvanesvari-Dhumavati	Space, manifest and unmanifest
Bhairavi-Bagalamukhi	Energy, in motion and in stillness

However, we should recognize that these terms have deeper meanings. Time to the yogi is not an abstract concept but the energy of eternal life. Space is not a mere vacuum but the presence of eternal love. The Word is no mere sound but the cosmic creative vibration. Light is the illumination power of consciousness itself. Energy is not a mere blind force but the very surge of Divine glory.

BENEFIC AND TERRIBLE FORMS

The Ten Forms of the Goddess are divided into two groups as benign and terrible. First is the terrible forms or the family of Kali, Kali-kula, which consists of Kali, Bhairavi, Chinnamasta, Bagala, and Dhumavati. Second is the benefic forms or the family of Shri, Shri-kula, led by Sundari, which consists of Sundari, Bhuvaneshvari, Matangi, and Kamala. Tara falls in between with her dark blue (nila) form being malefic, and her white form being benefic. This idea of terrible and beneficent Goddesses goes back to the *Vedas*, wherein the Goddesses have both their beauty (ornaments) and martial forms (weapons).

The benefic forms of the Goddess are more commonly worshipped along the right-handed path and the terrible forms along the left-handed path, but this distinction is very general. Both forms are necessary and complementary. The terrible forms remove ignorance and the beneficent forms give knowledge. However, unless ignorance is first removed we cannot benefit by knowledge.

Based on the fire and water (Agni-Soma) orientation of the *Vedas*, the terrible forms of Hindu deities relate to fire, lightning, and the sun, which are hot and destructive. The benefic forms relate to water and the moon, which are cooling and creative. Both elements are necessary. Fire is what cooks or ripens things. Water is the element that is cooked or transformed.

KALI, TARA, AND SUNDARI

Of the Ten Wisdom Goddesses, the first three are generally the most important. Kali represents power (shakti), Tara wisdom (prajña), and Sundari beauty (sundara), which are the three prime aspects of the Goddess. Kali relates to Shiva or the destroyer, while Tara has a connection with Brahma or the creator, and Sundari with Vishnu or the preserver. Kali is being or Sat, Tara is consciousness or Cit, and Sundari is bliss or Ananda, which constitute the threefold nature of the Absolute.

This takes us through the full scope of the Ten Great Knowledge Forms of the Mother. We have seen the most frightening and most lovely aspects of the Divine nature that both pervade the entire universe and exist within us as our true Self. We have only indicated the primary features of the great Goddesses. Much more will be revealed to the intuition of those who meditate upon them. The more we examine the Wisdom Goddesses, the more we discover their many levels of interrelationship and correspondence, both with each other and with all cosmic principles.

However, the Ten Wisdom Goddesses do not exhaust all the forms of the Mother, nor do they constitute all the important Hindu Goddesses.

Some great Goddesses are included indirectly in the Ten, like Durga who closely resembles Bhairavi. Others like Parvati, the loving wife of Shiva, are not specifically mentioned. The Ten Wisdom Goddesses are guides for meditation using the Mother as the primary deity, but she has other forms and functions related to her consort and her children, like her role as the mother of Ganesha and Skanda, the two sons of Parvati and Shiva.

PART III

THE PRACTICE OF TANTRIC YOGA

Where the fire (Agni) is enkindled, where the breath (Vayu) is controlled, where the nectar (Soma) overflows, there the Mind is born.

By the impulse of the Divine Sun, you should delight in the original Reality.
— *Shvetasavatara Upanishad II.6–7*

He who by discernment has effaced all objectivity is one established in the Reality of Awareness. He is the Fire of Awareness (Agni) and the wielder of the vajra (Indra). He is the Hero who has done away with death, canceling time itself.
— *Ramana Maharshi, Supplement to Reality in Forty Verses, verse 23*

1
TANTRIC YOGA
The Science of Psycho-physical Transformation

It is one thing to read about a teaching, but quite another to practice it. A theoretical examination serves as a basis for practice, or it may be useful in itself for expanding our mental horizons. Yet practice is something more and opens up an entirely different dimension of the teaching. It also requires a more detailed and technical knowledge. Having already examined the underlying principles of Tantric Yoga, in the following section we will examine its practices.

Please note that this information is not intended to function as a complete manual of Tantric practice. The subject of Yoga is complex and each individual must be treated differently. Additional guidance — whether from a teacher or from right intuition — will be necessary. Along with the primary mantric and meditational methods of Tantric Yoga, the use of diet, herbs and gems as aids to practice has been outlined. Hence those who are already practicing Yoga can benefit from this knowledge, as can those who follow the Ayurvedic system of medicine which is an important part of this tradition.

Yoga in its true sense is a science of meditation. The system of Tantric Yoga is not centered on Yoga postures, though these are helpful aids. There will be no examination of Yogic postures in this section, as such information is readily available elsewhere.

To understand the practice of Tantra we shall begin with a discussion of the internal energies that come into play in the practice of Yoga, which affect the physical body and the mind in extraordinary ways. Yoga is not concerned with the physical body or the mind in their ordinary states, but with bringing them into a quiescent condition so that they no longer obstruct the consciousness of the Self, in which alone there is liberation.

THE THREE BODIES

In the Vedic and Tantric system, the human being is regarded as composed of three "bodies," which function as vehicles for the inner Self or Purusha. Each body is a kind of matter or vibratory field which encloses the underlying consciousness; hence they are all called bodies. However, they are not all bodies in the physical sense. The inmost of the bodies, the causal body, is composed entirely of thought. The Tantric system is based on the Sankhya system of philosophy, which is presented here.

The Gross or Physical Body

The gross body (sthula sharira) is what we ordinarily regard as the physical body. It has sixteen components, which come in four groups:

1. Five sense organs: ear, skin, eye, tongue, and nose
2. Five organs of action: the vocal organ, hand, feet, the organ of elimination, and reproductive organ
3. Five elements: ether, air, fire, water and earth
4. The mind, which oversees and coordinates the sense organs and organs of action as the sixth sense organ

The first three sets of five factors correspond. For example, the ear, the vocal organ, and the element of ether relate to each other as correspondent sense organ, organ of action and element. The ear is the sense organ that perceives the element of ether. The vocal organ is the organ of action that works with it.

The physical body originates in the sexual union of the parents. It is built up and sustained by food. Within it the biological forces of the three humors (Vata, Pitta and Kapha or air, fire and water) operate as its main energies. This is the body that we normally experience, and our awareness within it constitutes the waking state of consciousness.

The Subtle or Astral Body

Within the physical is a subtle body of like form called the subtle or astral body (sukshma sharira). It is the "pure form" or energetic basis of the physical body. The subtle body is similarly composed of the sixteen components of the five sense organs, the five organs of action, the five elements, and the mind, but on a subtle level.

Psychic ability or E.S.P. derives from the functioning of the astral organs, which are not limited like the physical organs. The astral eye can see at a distance, the astral ear can hear at a distance, and so on. Similarly the astral organs of action allow action at a distance.

Each of the gross elements contains all of the five astral elements. The subtle body is composed of the simple elements only. For this reason the subtle body is lighter, freer and more active than the physical (for example, it can easily float or fly in astral space). It is composed of Prana or life-energy, which circulates through it as a subtle fluid of many colors.

In the subtle body exist the seven chakras or astral centers, with the force of Kundalini or the serpent power at the base allowing their full activation. There is an entire astral universe open for it to experience (the realm of pure form vibrant with color and vitality). In it, life is experienced as pure energy free of the inertia of gross matter. Astral objects take on the form of the mind which perceives them, and everything in the astral universe is perceived to be alive as an energy flow.

The astral world is experienced in dream, vision and trance. After death we sojourn in the astral world, which we may experience (according to our karma) as various positive or negative, heaven or hell-like states, as the subtle energies accumulated during physical life get released. Artists can access the astral realm during life, as it contains the pure or esthetic forms of things. The great devotional heavens of the Gods and Goddesses stand at the summit of the astral universe and to them their devotees ascend at death.

The Causal Body or Karmic Sheath

Within the subtle body is a yet more subtle body called the causal body (karana sharira) as it is the cause or creative force behind the other two. The causal body is not actually a body but a higher mind. Through it the soul can envision various experiences but is never really embodied in the physical or astral sense. The causal body is shaped like an egg around the other two bodies. It is composed of seven factors:

The Five Tanmatras
1. Smell, Gandha Tanmatra
2. Taste, Rasa Tanmatra
3. Sight, Rupa Tanmatra
4. Touch, Sparsha Tanmatra
5. Sound, Shabda Tanmatra

The Two Components of the Causal Mind
6. Ego, Ahamkara
7. Intellligence, Buddhi

The Tanmatras are the causal elements, the root materials from which the subtle and gross sense organs, organs of actions and the elements all evolve, and the common factor which allows their interconnection. Through the Tanmatras the causal body creates the experiences of the other two bodies. Through the Tanmatras it has the power to create whatever object or quality it wishes, as all objects or organs are nothing but combinations of the Tanmatras. Once yogis come to master the Tanmatras they learn all the secrets of nature. The causal body stores the seeds or impressions of karma that motivate us from birth to birth and is thus the reincarnating entity or karmic sheath. The individual soul (Jivatman) is the being that functions relative to this body.

The causal mind is itself a modification of the Tanmatras on a more refined level. The seven components of the causal body produce all the factors that make up the other two bodies.

The causal body has the causal universe open to it (the formless realm of Divine truth principles) and can experience all creation as the manifestation of its own meditations, including creating universes of its own. The causal body is a kind of supermind, in which we partake of the Divine mind and all its creative and transformative powers. Normally we only touch upon the causal body in deep sleep, profound perception, or deep silence of mind. We must return to the causal body every night in deep sleep, as it alone is the source of life-energy through which the other bodies are revitalized.

The causal body is centered in the heart, which is not the Heart Chakra of the astral or physical body, but the spiritual heart slightly to the right of the center of the chest (see below).

PRIMAL MATTER AND THE SELF

Beyond the causal body there are two factors:

Prakriti or Primal Nature

Prakriti is the subtle substance out of which the different bodies are built. It is the essential material of all experience and contains all possible properties that we come to experience in objects. It is composed of three primal qualities, the three gunas of Sattva (harmony), Rajas (turbulence) and Tamas (resistance). These three gunas create the three bodies: Sattva creating the causal, Rajas the astral, and Tamas the physical. The five Tanmatras reflected on the three gunas create the five sense organs (from Sattva), the five organs of action (from Rajas), and the five elements (from Tamas).

Prakriti is extremely subtle. Even the mind is a product of it. Thought cannot reach it. Yet it contains the seed of objectivity and hence can be perceived by pure consciousness as the most subtle object of perception.

Atman or Purusha, the Self

Atman or the Self is the pure consciousness beyond all objects, worlds, bodies, and experiences. This true Self is not the ego (ahamkara), which is a modification of the mind, but Awareness itself. The Self contains its Shakti or power of vision, which is not separate and is the source of Prakriti.

BRAHMAN, THE ABSOLUTE

Purusha and Prakriti, or Spirit and Nature, are one in Brahman or the Absolute, which is the substance of all existence as well as the power of all consciousness. All yogic practices are devised to return us to the Self which is the Absolute. Brahman is the ultimate reality or pure being in all existence, objective or subjective, in which there is perfect peace.

Prakriti is related to Maya, the power of illusion, and to Shakti, the power of consciousness. Prakriti refers to the basic substance of experience, the power that allows objects to appear. Maya is the power that makes the One appear as Many. Ignorance (Avidya) is the power that hides the reality of the One and makes us see multiplicity as real. Shakti is the power of consciousness which removes ignorance and reveals the sole reality of the Self. Maya or Prakriti are in essence one with Atman-Brahman as its inherent power of creation.

THE FIVE SHEATHS AND THE SEVEN LEVELS OF EXISTENCE

The three bodies consist of various layers, explained in the *Upanishads* as five sheaths.

1. Food sheath, Annamaya kosha
2. Breath sheath, Pranamaya kosha
3. Mind sheath, Manomaya kosha
4. Intelligence sheath, Vijñanamaya kosha
5. Bliss sheath, Anandamaya kosha

The physical body is composed primarily of the food sheath; the astral body is composed primarily of the mind sheath; and the causal body of the bliss sheath. The breath sheath serves to mediate between the physical and astral bodies. The intelligence sheath mediates between the astral and causal bodies. In addition are two more cosmic principles, making seven in all.

6. Consciousness, Cit
7. Being, Sat

These last two are often correlated with bliss or ananda as the triple principle of Sacchidananda or Being-Consciousness-Bliss which represents the Absolute.

THE SEVEN CHAKRAS

The practical techniques of Yoga involve awakening the energy of the subtle body called the Kundalini, the coiled energy or serpent force. The subtle body is composed of seven chakras or energy centers. Chakra means "what revolves" and hence signifies a wheel. The chakras are also called lotuses, as they are shaped like flowers and composed of different petals. Each petal of a chakra relates to one of the prime letters of the Sanskrit alphabet. Each chakra governs a certain element, sense organ, organ of action, Prana (life-force), and function of the mind. Each has a physical counterpart through a physiological system, nerve plexus and endocrine organ.

Below is an outline of the seven chakras and their function. To avoid misinterpretations we will name the chakras after their respective elements, rather than after their location in the physical body, which may cause us to confuse the chakras with their physical counterparts.

1. Muladhara Chakra — Earth Chakra (Root)

The Earth Chakra or root center is located at the base of the spine. Muladhara means "root foundation."

The Earth Chakra has four petals consisting of the mantras vam, śam, ṣam, and sam. It is the seat of the earth element or solid state of matter, whose governing seed syllable (bija mantra) is Lam.

The Yogini (feminine power of Yoga) governing this chakra is Shakini, and among the seven tissues it relates to the bones.

It rules the sense organ of smell, the nose, and the organ of reproduction among the organs of action.

In the mind it relates to ego (ahamkara). It is associated with the downward moving of the vital energies (Apana Vayu).

In the physical body, it corresponds to the sacral plexus and to the urino-genital system. In the endocrine system its counterparts are the ovaries and testes.

Its elemental symbol is a yellow square. The color of the chakra itself is deep crimson red.

2. Svadhishthana Chakra — Water Chakra (Sex Center)

The Water Chakra is often called the "sex center" as it is located just above the root center in the region of the sex organs. This name, however, is a misnomer. Technically, the origin of the sexual energy comes from the previous chakra. While the physical counterpart of this chakra is still associated with sexual energy, this chakra itself is concerned with the water energy as a whole. Its Sanskrit name means the self-abode, as it is here where the Kundalini energy resides when coiled or hidden.

The Water Chakra possesses six petals consisting of the mantras bam, bham, mam, yam, ram, and lam. It is the seat of the water element or liquid state of matter, whose governing seed syllable is vam.

The Yogini governing this chakra is Kakini, and it relates to fat or adipose tissue among the seven tissues.

It rules the sense organ of taste, the tongue, and the organ of action of elimination among the organs of action.

Relative to the mind, it refers to the sensate mind or emotional principle (manas), which works through the senses. It is associated with the inward moving of the vital energies (Prana Vayu).

Relative to the physical body it corresponds to the coccyx and to the urinogenital system. In the endocrine system its counterparts are the adrenals.

Its elemental symbols is a white crescent. The color of the chakra itself is dark blue.

3. Manipura Chakra — Fire Chakra (Navel)

The Fire Chakra is often called the navel center as it is located behind the navel. Manipura means "the city of gems," as this chakra is radiant like a city of jewels.

The Fire Chakra possesses ten petals consisting of the mantras ḍam, ḍham, ṇam, tam, tham, dam, dham, nam, pam, and pham. It is the seat of the fire element or radiant state of matter, whose governing seed syllable is Ram.

The Yogini governing this chakra is Lakini, and among the seven tissues it relates to muscle.

It rules the sense organ of sight, the eyes, and the feet (movement) among the organs of action.

In the mind it relates to the reasoning faculty (buddhi). It is associated with the upward moving of the vital energies (Udana Vayu).

In the physical body, it corresponds to the solar plexus and to the digestive system (particularly the liver and small intestine). Of the endocrine glands its counterpart is the pancreas.

Its elemental symbol is a red downward pointing triangle. The color of the chakra itself is dark blue.

4. Anahata Chakra — Air Chakra (Heart)

The Air Chakra is often called the heart center as it is located along the spine at the level of the heart. Anahata means "unstruck sound," as it is from here that inner sounds or natural music (Nada) of the subtle body arises.

The Air Chakra has twelve petals consisting of the mantras kam, kham, gam, gham, nam, cam, cham, jam, jham, ñam, tam, and tham. It is the seat of the element of air or the gaseous state of matter, whose governing seed syllable is Yam.

The Yogini governing this chakra is Rakini, and among the seven tissues it relates to the blood.

It rules the sense organ of touch, the skin, and the hands (grasping) among the organs of action.

In the mind it relates to the conditioned consciousness as a whole (citta). It is the seat of the diffusive air or vital energy (Vyana Vayu), though governing over the element of air it has an influence on all the Pranas.

In the physical body it corresponds to the heart plexus and to the circulatory system. In the endocrine system its counterpart is the thymus gland.

Its elemental symbol is a smoky colored six pointed star or seal of Solomon. The color of the chakra itself is deep red.

5. Vishuddha Chakra — Ether Chakra (Throat)

The Ether Chakra is often called the throat center. Vishuddha means "very pure," as this center is very subtle.

The Ether Chakra has sixteen petals consisting of the vowels of the Sanskrit alphabet: am, ām, im, īm, um, ūm, ṛm, ṝm, lrm, ḷrm, em, aim, om, aum, am, and aḥ. It is the seat of space, the element of ether or the etheric state of matter, whose governing seed syllable is Ham.

The Yogini governing this chakra is Dakini, and among the seven tissues it relates to the plasma.

It rules the organ of sound, the ears, and the vocal organ (mouth) among the organs of action.

It is the site of the individual soul (jiva) and is the source of inspiration. It is the seat of the balancing air or vital force (Samana Vayu).

In the physical body it relates to the throat and larynx and to the respiratory system. In the endocrine system its counterpart is the thyroid.

Its elemental symbol is a dark blue circle. The color of the chakra itself is a smoky grey.

6. Ajña Chakra — Third Eye

Called the Third Eye, this is the Mind Chakra. Ajña means "command" and this is called the center of command, as from here the other chakras are guided.

The Third Eye has two petals (by some accounts forty-eight), consisting of the mantras ham and khsham. It is the seat of the mind-space or mental ether (which underlies the elemental ether). Its seed syllable is ksham, meaning patience, peace and fortitude.

The Yogini governing this chakra is Hakini, and it relates to the nerve tissue among the seven tissues.

It rules the mind as both a sense organ and organ of action. It is the seat of the primary Prana or life-force.

In the mind it is the site of the cosmic or universal Self and the center from which we have direct contact with the Divine Creator and ruler of the universe (Ishvara).

In the physical body it relates to the cerebellum and medulla oblongata and governs the involuntary nervous system. In the endocrine system its counterpart is the pituitary gland.

Its elemental symbol is a point. The color of the chakra is silver white.

7. Sahasra Padma Chakra — Crown Chakra (Head Center)

Called the head center according to its position, its Sanskrit name means "the thousand-petaled lotus." It is the center of pure consciousness. For practical purposes it can be called the Crown Chakra and is also symbolized by a crown.

The Crown Chakra has a thousand petals and is the seat of the spirit (Atman or Purusha). Its seed syllable is Om. It is the seat of consciousness or consciousness-space that is the origin of the mental and material ethers.

The Yogini governing this chakra is Yakini, and it relates to the reproductive fluid among the seven tissues.

In the mind it is the site of the supreme Self (Paramatman). As the seat of the true Self it is the source and guide of all the energies of the body, the essence of life itself.

In the physical body it relates to the cerebrum and governs the voluntary nervous system. In the endocrine system it functions through the pineal gland.

It is without symbol or color.

THE NADIS

The subtle body, like the physical, consists of various channel-systems called "nadis," which literally means streams. Seventy-two thousand nadis are said to exist. Of these, fourteen are significant, and three are most important.

The Sushumna

Most significant of the nadis is the Sushumna, which runs through the center of the astral spine and corresponds to the spinal canal in the physical body. The chakras are strung like lotuses upon it. The Sushumna has the nature of fire and is activated by the Kundalini.

The Ida and Pingala

To the left and right of the Sushumna run two major nadis whose movement intertwines (like a series of figure eights put one on top of the other, as in a caduceus). These start at the base of the spine and move from side to side, chakra to chakra. The left nadi ends at the left nostril, the right nadi at the right nostril.

The left nadi is called the Ida or lunar nadi, as it has the energy of the Moon. It is white in color, feminine, has a watery (Kapha) nature, and is cool, wet and soothing. Ida means literally inspiration, refreshment. It operates more during the night and promotes sleep. Psychologically it promotes emotion, feeling, love and attachment.

The right nadi is called the Pingala or solar nadi, as it has the energy of the Sun. Pingala means red. It is masculine, has a fiery (Pitta) nature, and is hot, dry and stimulating. It operates more during the day and promotes activity. Psychologically it promotes reason, perception, analysis and discrimination. Normally the breath flows in one of these two channels, alternating every few hours according to various factors of time, environment and constitution.

There are five other important nadis, running from the sense organs to the third eye, making seven nadis total for the head. Each of the two ears has a nadi, as does each of the two eyes. An additional nadi, called the Sarasvati, runs from the tongue and is responsible for the power of speech. Additional nadis bring Prana to the right hand and foot, left hand and foot, the organs of elimination, the urinary organs, the digestive organs, and the skin, making fourteen major nadis in all. The yogi may experience the flow of Prana or vital energy through all these channels.

Additional Chakras

There are several minor chakras, including those of the hands and the feet. Some teachings speak of additional chakras above the head. Actually all the astral chakras are above or beyond the physical head and are generally experienced through the Third Eye. There are residual chakras below the spine. But for the main purposes of Tantric Yoga the seven chakras are considered to be the most important.

THE FIVE PRANAS IN THE SUBTLE BODY

The life-force or Prana is divided fivefold according to its movement and function. The five Pranas have their action on the subtle body, which it is important to know. This somewhat different than their functions in the physical body. Both factors are listed below:

1. SAMANA VAYU, the equalizing breath — dwelling in the navel and responsible for digestion in the physical body — relates to the element of ether in the subtle body from its abode in the Throat Chakra, and creates space, balance, equilibrium and equanimity for the mind. Its mental function corresponds to the individual Self (Jivata-man).

2. VYANA VAYU, the diffusive breath — pervading the entire body and responsible for movement of the limbs and circulation in the physical body — relates to air in the subtle body from its abode in the Heart Chakra and gives motion, pervasion and comprehension to the mind. Its mental function corresponds to feeling (Citta).

3. UDANA VAYU, the ascending breath — located in the throat and responsible for speech in the physical body — relates to fire in the subtle body, and from its abode in the Fire Chakra gives the power of perception, discrimination, and the ability to ascend in consciousness. Its mental function corresponds to reason (Buddhi).

4. PRANA VAYU, the inward moving breath — located in the heart and brain and responsible for inhalation in the physical body — relates to water in the subtle body, and from its abode in the Water Chakra and gives the capacity to absorb sensations, feelings, and thoughts in the mind. Its mental function corresponds to emotion (Manas).

5. APANA VAYU, the downward moving breath — located in the lower centers in the physical body and responsible for elimination — relates to earth in the subtle body, and from its abode in the Earth Chakra gives the capacity to hold, support and maintain resistance in the mind. Its mental function corresponds to ego (Ahamkara).

For developing higher consciousness we must be attuned to these higher Pranic forces. As their energies develop we will experience peace of mind (samana), expansion of mind (vyana), ascension of energy (udana), interiorization of energy (prana), and warding off of negative energy (apana).

Udana Vayu brings about the upward movement of the Kundalini through the Sushumna. Vyana Vayu allows the opening of the peripheral channels of the subtle body and the heart. Samana Vayu creates a guiding equilibrium and equanimity during the process. Prana Vayu maintains the balance of fluids. Apana Vayu allows us to ward off negative energies and eliminate negative emotions. It also allows the subtle body to separate from the physical body.

BEYOND THE ASTRAL BODY
The Two Heart Centers

According to great teachers like Ramana Maharshi and Ganapati Muni, there are two heart centers. The first is the heart center of the subtle body or Anahata Chakra, which is the center of sound vibration or Nada. The second is the spiritual heart or center of the causal body, located at the right side of the chest. From it one can directly experience all the powers of the causal body. Yet this heart center transcends the causal body as the center of awareness beyond duality. This center should not be confused with the astral heart chakra, which has a devotional nature and may still be attached to some form or concept. The higher or spiritual heart (hridaya) is emphasized in Vedantic teachings as the seat of liberation.

Amrita Nadi

There is another part of the Sushumna or central channel, apart from its normal course that runs from the Root to the Crown Chakra. An additional channel descends from the Crown Chakra to the spiritual heart center. It is called Amrita Nadi, the "immortal channel," or Atma Nadi, "the channel of the Self." It is said to be the key to Self-realization. Dwelling on the Atman keeps our energy in the Amrita Nadi. This requires divesting the mind of objectivity and seeing the universe as consciousness only.

All that yogis accomplish through taking the Kundalini up through the seven chakras can be experienced by Jñanis, yogis of the path of wisdom, by dwelling on the spiritual heart alone.

2
OPENING
THE CHAKRAS

*From the thousand-petalled to the two-petalled lotus,
and from the two-petalled lotus back to the thousand, from
the thousand-petalled lotus to the entire body, the Goddess
Consciousness travels through our entire range of experience.*

*From the thousand-petalled lotus to the two-petalled
lotus, from the two-petalled lotus to the hidden lotus of the
heart, those for whom the Queen of the Universe descends,
for them is eternal adherence in their own nature.*

*Thus turning from the body into the most inward state,
or into the root center and abode of Kundalini, those of
steady wisdom gain the eternal adherence in their own
nature.* — *Ganapati Muni, Uma Sahasram 38. 3, 6, 7*

The key to Tantric Yoga is to awaken the Kundalini and open the
chakras. This unfolds the powers of the subtle and causal bodies and
connects us with our true nature. Tantric teachings speak of the movement
of the Kundalini from the base of the spine up through the six chakras to
the head in order to bring about Self-realization. Along this route the
Kundalini unfolds the powers of each chakra that it passes through.

Opening a chakra gives an understanding of the respective element
and organ that it rules and its universal meaning. We come to understand
the cosmic elements and organs as the powers behind all manifestation
and merge our world-idea into consciousness, ultimately coming to
understand our own Self as the sole reality.

SIGNS OF OPENED CHAKRAS
Earth Chakra

Opening the Earth Chakra frees us from the idea that solid matter is
real. One perceives the cosmic earth element and its attributes as the sole
reality behind all solid forms. One gains mastery over the sense of smell
and realizes that all fragrances are manifestations of the cosmic principle
of smell. One similarly gains mastery over the organ of reproduction and

Dakshinamurti is the youthful form of Lord Shiva as the silent teacher. He is the consort of youthful Sundari, the third of the Ten Wisdom Goddesses.

Om Dakṣiṇāmūrtaye namaḥ!

realizes that behind every reproductive urge in the universe is the cosmic action of procreation.

The downward moving air (Apana Vayu) is awakened on a subtle level, giving the ability to ward off negative thoughts and emotions. One realizes the cosmic Apana Vayu as the real power behind the downward movement of energy in the universe. The body and mind become light and the amount of waste material produced by the body becomes less. A pure fragrance issues from the body.

Water Chakra

Opening the Water Chakra frees us from the idea that liquid matter is real. One perceives the cosmic water element and its attributes as the sole reality behind all liquid forms. One gains mastery over the sense of taste and realizes that all taste sensations are manifestations of the cosmic principle of taste. One similarly gains mastery over the organ of elimination. One realizes that behind every purification function in the universe is the cosmic action of purification.

The inward moving air (Prana Vayu) is awakened on a subtle level, giving the ability to interiorize our energy. One realizes the cosmic Prana Vayu as the real power behind the inward movement of energy in the universe. The body and mind become fluid, adaptable and pure.

Fire Chakra

Opening the Fire Chakra frees us from the idea that radiant matter is real. One perceives the cosmic fire element and its attributes as the sole reality behind all radiant forms. One gains mastery over the sense of sight and realizes that all light sensations are manifestations of the cosmic principle of light. One similarly gains mastery over the organ of motion (the feet). One realizes that behind every action of movement in the universe is the cosmic function of movement.

The upward moving air (Udana Vayu) is awakened on a subtle level, giving mastery over all ascending movements of energy. One understands the cosmic Udana Vayu as the real power behind ascending energy in the universe. The body and mind thus become radiant, with a strong luster to the skin and the eyes.

Air Chakra

Opening the Air Chakra frees us from the idea that gaseous matter is real. One perceives the cosmic air element and its attributes as the sole reality behind all gaseous forms. One gains mastery over the sense of touch and realizes that all touch sensations are manifestations of the cosmic principle of vibration. One similarly gains mastery over the manual organ. One realizes that behind the all shaping actions in the universe is the cosmic function of making things.

The expansive air (Vyana Vayu) is awakened on a subtle level, giving an understanding of all expansive movements of energy. One realizes the cosmic Vyana Vayu as the real power behind expanding energy in the universe. The body and mind thus become expansive.

Ether Chakra

Opening the Ether Chakra frees us from the idea that etheric matter is real. One perceives the cosmic ether element and its attributes as the sole reality behind all space. One gains mastery over the sense of hearing and realizes that all hearing sensations are manifestations of the cosmic principle of sound. One similarly gains mastery over the vocal organ. One realizes that behind all organs of expression in the universe, like the human vocal organs, is the cosmic function of expression and articulation.

The balancing air (Samana Vayu) is awakened on a subtle level, giving an understanding of all regulating movements of energy. One realizes the cosmic Samana Vayu as the real power behind the regulation of energy in the universe. The body and mind become ethereal and there is a feeling of voidness and infinite space.

Third Eye

Opening the Third Eye frees us from the idea that the mind is real. One perceives the cosmic mind element as the sole reality behind all mental forms. One gains mastery over the mind and comes to have a continual stream of Divine perceptions. One realizes that everything we think is a manifestation of the cosmic principle of mind.

The chief Prana or primary life-force is awakened on a subtle level. One comes to understand the One Life-Force behind all the movements of energy in the universe, animate and inanimate. The sense of a separate mind and body disappears.

Crown Chakra

Opening the Crown Chakra frees us from the idea that there is any reality apart from the Self. One perceives cosmic consciousness as the sole reality behind all forms of consciousness.One gains mastery over consciousness and comes to abide in a state of Self-realization. One realizes that all appearances are only forms of one's own Self. One realizes all the universe as pure awareness. The sense of a separate self disappears into the realization of the One Self in all beings.

MANIFESTATIONS OF THE SUBTLE SENSE ORGANS

The awakened chakras are primarily indicated by the ability to understand their respective elements, sense organs, organs of action, and Pranas according to their cosmic nature. It is possible through the opened chakras to have experiences of these organs as well.

The Earth Chakra through the subtle organ of smell allows us to perceive celestial or astral fragrances. The Water Chakra through the subtle organ of taste allows us to perceive heavenly or astral tastes. The Fire Chakra through the subtle organ of sight allows us to perceive astral lights. The Air Chakra through the subtle organ of touch allows us to perceive astral vibrations. The Ether Chakra through the subtle organ of hearing allows us to perceive astral sounds.

The Earth Chakra through the subtle organ of reproduction allows us to experience the cosmic action of creation. The Water Chakra through the subtle organ of elimination allows us to perceive the cosmic action of dissolution. The Fire Chakra through the subtle organ of motion allows us to enter into the cosmic movement of expansion. The Air Chakra through the subtle organ of formation allows us to understand the formative processes of the universe. The Ether Chakra through the subtle organ of speech allows us to participate in the Divine Word.

These subtle experiences cannot be gained by a mind attached to sensation, as the attachment of the mind to the gross or outer sensory potentials renders it too heavy to perceive these finer vibrations. To experience the subtle organs we must have detachment from the gross organs.

Variations

While this is the general movement, there are many variations. The Kundalini can be awakened from any chakra, providing that we can direct the full concentration of the mind upon it. Direct yogic practices, emphasizing formless meditation or Self-inquiry, awaken it through the third eye or the spiritual heart. Devotional approaches work primarily with the Heart Chakra of the astral body. Nor is experiencing all the powers of the chakras necessary. Direct yogic approaches keep the energy in the Sushumna. Such yogis gain the mastery of the energies of each chakra but may not explore the faculties or worlds of experience each chakra relates to. Yogis who have no desire for the experience of the subtle organs or worlds will not have them. They understand how the elements, organs and Pranas are all aspects of consciousness itself. Experiencing that consciousness directly, they do not need to examine its manifestations, just as the ocean is not interested in the movement of its waves.

MISINTERPRETATIONS OF THE CHAKRAS

Much of New Age thought tends to identify the chakras with their physical counterparts. For example, if a person is highly emotional, it may be said that he or she has an open Heart Chakra. If a person has high sexual energy, he or she is said to have a strong Sex Chakra. Such statements relate to the physical functions which are reflections of the unopened astral chakras, not to the chakras in their opened condition. The chakras themselves become active only when the mind and Prana have entered into the Sushumna. This requires concentrated yogic practices and does not occur during ordinary consciousness.

According to yogic texts the chakras are closed in all people except those who have practiced deep meditation. The result of this is not disease or psychological discomfort but spiritual ignorance, however physically healthy or emotionally happy we may happen to be. The opening of the chakras is not done to cure disease or release blocked emotions but to merge the mind in the state of Samadhi, wherein the sense of separate self disappears into the One Self of all.

It is possible to partially open the lower chakras (those below the heart) before they have been purified properly. This can lead to an exaggeration of ordinary human drives, like excessive anger or sexuality. But this should not be confused with a proper and wholesome opening of these force centers, in which such extreme manifestations will occur only in a very transient and limited manner, if at all.

The chakras are misinterpreted when we look at them primarily on a physical level. For example, sexual activity is a function of the physical organs. It is not the function of the awakened Earth or Water Chakras, which give detachment from the organs of reproduction and elimination. Increasing the activity of the physical organs does not aid in developing the chakras but depresses their function, as their energy is directed outwardly and into physical matter, not into the inner consciousness.

The function of the awakened lower chakras is not to promote the activity of their corresponding physical organs but to bring them under the control of consciousness. Once we realize that what we are seeking outwardly is a manifestation of the elements inherent in our own consciousness, we will no longer desire anything from the external world.

The awakening of the astral chakras does bring about changes in the physical body. However, most of these are subjective. They change our perception of the physical body and our relationship to it. We cease seeing the body as our true self and come to see it as the gross vehicle or outer encasement for the soul. The physical body becomes pure, light, and full of energy and radiance. The mind becomes free of desire, fear, anger, stress and anxiety.

Yoga shows us how to open the chakras. However, the opening of the chakras is a by-product of the practice, not an end in itself. The goal is not the opening of the chakras, which is a mere technical matter, but realization of our true nature, in which alone is the peace and happiness that we are really seeking. To be more concerned about the particularities of the chakras than with realizing our true nature is like being more concerned about the physiology of the stomach than with the quality of the food that we are eating.

Astral Travel and the Occult

Astral experiences, like "astral travel" (flying in one's astral body), do not necessarily indicate the opening of the chakras. They occur as part of the ordinary functioning of the astral body, as experienced in dream and after death states. Similarly, one can have contact with the astral realm or gain occult knowledge without a clear awakening of the inner consciousness. The chakras are only fully opened when we comprehend the reality of the cosmic principles behind them. They are not part of ordinary astral activity but of merging the astral body and mind into the consciousness which transcends all embodiment.

The chakras up to the navel can be used by a subtle concentrated ego. It is said that even the demons (beings of egoistic energy) practice Yoga up to this level. Even this requires much concentration, discipline, and austerity. Such individuals may see through the limitations of the physical world and the ordinary ego, and thereby go beyond most human limitations, but still remain attached to their sense of achievement. It is possible to have a great deal of personal power, charisma or talent, including skill in manipulating people, without a real inner awakening. One can also speak of these internal energies without having really mastered them. Hence one should be careful not to confuse different skills and powers with the awakening of the chakras or real enlightenment.

We must discriminate between true opening of the chakras and merely experiencing an aspect of their heightened function. There are endless fascinating but fleeting subtle states that we can experience short of fully arousing the Kundalini. These can have a powerful effect upon the mind and go far beyond ordinary consciousness, yet they remain in a realm of illusion that can mislead us as to our real attainments.

It can be dangerous for one who is not properly trained or purified to try force these subtle energies. Even if such individuals succeed in moving the Kundalini or bringing the chakras into play, there will be something unwholesome about their experience. A subtle form of ego may persuade them to think that they are a prophet or messiah, that they alone have the Word of God, or that their thoughts and desires must be Divine. Many sectarian religious doctrines that exist in the world, the separate and warring creeds, have arisen from such untrained spiritual experiences, which were authentic but one-sided. Hence a balanced yogic tradition and science is crucial in all cultures. Proper understanding and training in it should precede or accompany any attempts to produce altered or expanded states of consciousness.

3
TANTRIC AND AYURVEDIC SCIENCE
Prana, Tejas and Ojas:
The Spiritual Energies of Air, Fire and Water

We have drunk the Soma. We have become immortal.
We have gone to the light and found the Gods. How can
the powers of illusion affect us now? Oh Immortal Bliss,
what can the harmful attitudes of mortals do to us any-
more? — *Rig Veda VIII.48.3*

He who drinks the nectar from the lotus of the head is
the sinless Self-contained drinker of the Soma. His fire
sacrifice (Agnihotra), oh Queen of All, on the altar of the
root chakra is eternal.
— *Ganapati Muni, Uma Sahasram. 15.10*

To understand Tantric Yoga we must also examine the knowledge of
Ayurveda. Ayurveda is not only a medical system for ordinary healing
purposes, it also shows us how the subtle energies of the body and mind
function in the practice of Yoga. As such it can help us awaken these
energies properly and keep them in balance. Practicing Tantric Yoga on
an Ayurvedic basis and with Ayurvedic health regimens greatly facilitates
its efficacy.

I. AGNI AND SOMA: THE KEY TO YOGIC PROCESSES
All Vedic and yogic science — whether Ayurveda, Vedic astrology
or Yoga — revolves around the two fundamental principles of Agni and
Soma. This is also true of Tantra.

Agni and Soma are, as it were, the yin and yang of yogic thought.
Like yin and yang they relate to a series of opposites that apply on many
different levels, which in fact encompass the basic duality behind all
existence. We are not going to examine all the complex correlations of
Agni and Soma, but will restrict ourselves to those relevant to the practice
of Yoga.

Agni is literally fire. Yet Agni is not only the element of fire but all that can be symbolically associated with fire: heat, energy, austerity, and illumination, including ultimately awareness itself. Agni brings about growth, expansion, ascension, and transformation. It is the fire hidden in earthly things which rises out of them to heaven beyond. Hence Agni is the spirit hidden in matter, or consciousness hidden in its material vestures.

Soma, as the opposite of Agni, relates with the element of water or the liquid state of matter, whose light form is the Moon. Soma is cooling, consolidating, and conserving in its activity. As Agni is the eater or enjoyer, Soma is associated with food and hence all that can be enjoyed. Soma means nectar or ambrosia, amrit, which also means the "immortal." It refers to whatever causes us to swell with joy and thereby allows our essence to stream forth. The joy of generation and creation are part of the joy of Soma. Yet Soma is more; it is the beauty and the joy of meditation, when our inner essence, the delight of consciousness, stands revealed.

Agni and Soma and Sexual Energy

Yoga works with sexual energy not for ordinary enjoyment or procreation but for the illumining of consciousness. In this regard Agni or fire relates to the female energy or Shakti. Soma or water is the male energy or Shiva. The male sexual energy or semen is lunar or cool, while the female sexual energy, which is red and relates to the blood, is fiery or hot. In alchemical terms the female sexual energy is sulphur, while the male energy is mercury. Yoga seeks to unite Agni and Soma or the female and male principles of our nature.

We should note, however, that the sexual energy is the opposite of normal bodily polarity. The male generally represents fire and the female is water, just as the male temperament is hotter or more aggressive and the female cooler or more receptive. In the reproductive systems these polarities are switched. This is because the sexual energy represents that portion of the opposite sex which is contained within us and which seeks to return to a being of like nature. The sexual fire in the female is the portion of male energy which is contained within her generally more watery nature. The sexual water of the male is similarly the portion of female energy contained within his generally more fiery nature. Each opposite contains within it the seed of its own opposite. Sexual desire seeks to restore the original state of unity.

Tantric Yoga focuses on the unification of male and female energies; this is the basis of the integration and transformation of the psyche. The outer forms of Tantric Yoga use male and female partners and actual sexual practices. The inner and more specifically yogic practices of Tantra unite the male and female energies within our own psyche and do not require any external partner.

Purifying Sexual Energy

Our sexual energies in their ordinary expression are not helpful for the practice of Yoga, because they are directed outward and can be mixed with impurities or toxins of various sorts. First, our sexual energies must be purified and made subtle. According to Ayurveda there are seven tissues that make up the body, which are produced from the food that is digested and assimilated:

1. plasma
2. blood
3. muscle
4. fat
5. bone
6. marrow and nerve tissue
7. reproductive tissue

Each of these tissues is a transformation of the previous one, like milk becoming butter. Each becomes less in substance but greater in potency. For example, plasma is greater in quantity than the reproductive fluid, but the reproductive fluid contains much more concentrated energy.

The reproductive fluid is the most potent ingredient in the body and the ultimate product of the digestive process. Though smaller in quantity than other bodily tissues, it has the greatest energy. It can produce new life and thus it also has the capacity to renew the life within the body itself. The energy of reproductive tissue is indispensable for achieving any internal transformation.

While ordinarily we direct the sexual energy outward for procreative or pleasure purposes, Yoga practice directs this energy inward for revitalization and the development of higher consciousness. For this inner process to take place the sexual energies must shift their location from their ordinary sites. It is not the outgoing sexual energies that are united but their subtle counterparts. If a sufficient amount of the reproductive fluid has not first been raised to the head and the energy of awareness has not been brought down to the base of the spine, we are not yet ready for the advanced practices of Yoga.

The reproductive fluid must be distilled, in which process it rises to the brain and becomes Soma. This requires the surrender of our desire for outer enjoyment, offering it into a fire of aspiration to discover the Divine within. Our Soma or desire for fulfillment must be redirected from its fixation on the outer world and the lower bodily centers to the Third Eye. Conversely Agni, the fire or power of perception and attention, must be directed from the head to the base of the spine, from its fixation on the outer world through the senses to its connection with the inner source of vitality. This requires calming the restless mind, withdrawing from sensory stimuli which keep our inquiring energy in the head, and discovering the deeper perception hidden at the root of the unconscious.

Many yogic practices are helpful to purify sexual energy. Particularly when combined with the cultivation of devotion, Asana (Yogic postures) and Pranayama (breathing exercises) can be used to help redirect the reproductive fluid upward. Mantra and meditation, and also music and chanting, help direct the mental fire inward and downward.

Nada and Bindu

Agni or fire relates to the Kundalini, which dwells at the base of the spine. Soma or the Moon relates to the immortal nectar, Amrit, which dwells in the Crown chakra. In Tantric Yoga the fire ascends and thereby melts the immortal nectar. When the fire reaches the Crown chakra it unites with Soma or the Moon, which is the union of Shiva and Shakti. The fire or Shakti arises to unite with the Soma or Shiva. To put it into simpler language, Agni or fire represents our spiritual aspiration, the ascending search of the mind for the Divine. Soma represents the descent of Divine grace. Both factors are necessary and each serves to complement and support the other.

Agni relates to Nada or the original sound vibration, which has an ascending motion. Soma relates to the Bindu or point-drop of pure awareness, which moves downward. The interplay of Nada and Bindu creates the universe. These again are Shakti and Shiva. Nada is also the feminine energy of intense devotion and aspiration and Bindu the masculine energy of clear, cool perception. Nada is increased by working with sound and mantra. Bindu is increased by working with perception and meditation.

Vayu: Air or Breath

Between the basic duality of Agni and Soma is a third principle. When two opposites unite, an offspring is created. Agni and Soma, as fire and water, unite to create Vayu, wind or air. The cosmic male and female forces, the father and the mother, unite to create a child, which is life or Prana. While in ordinary sexual activity the life created is outside oneself, in the practice of Yoga it is one's own inner or spiritual life energy that is created. A new dimension of life comes into being, a creative reality of consciousness beyond the limitations of physical form.

According to Tantra, Vayu dwells in the Heart Chakra, which is the chakra that relates to the element of air. The union of Agni and Soma opens and energizes this chakra. Tantra generally relates Agni to the first two chakras, the Earth and Water chakras. Vayu relates to the second two chakras of fire and air. Soma relates to the higher two chakras, those of ether and mind.

Surya: the Sun

After the three principles have come into function, there is a fourth or unitary principle which integrates them. Agni, Soma and Vayu are one in Surya: fire, water and air are one in the Sun, which represents the source of heat, rain, and vitality.

This supreme solar principle is both the origin and the end of the three principles, as well as the center around which their movements take place. According to the *Vedas* the Self or Atman dwells as the Sun within the heart or center of our being. Hence the ultimate Yoga and the supreme Tantric Yoga is the Yoga of the Sun, which aims to manifest the Divine Light of consciousness, the Sun of Suns within us.

II. PRANA, TEJAS AND OJAS:
THE SPIRITUAL ENERGIES OF AIR, FIRE AND WATER

Having examined the basic principles of yogic science, we can now examine the energies of the mind and subtle body on a more detailed level. For this we must bring in the concepts of Ayurveda or yogic medicine. Ayurveda not only teaches us about the physical body, it also relates to the subtle body, whose energies are based on the same cosmic and biological principles. Much of the practical foundation for Tantra can be found in Ayurveda, while the higher practices of Ayurveda are related to Tantra.

Ayurveda is based on the Tridosha theory, the concept of the three biological humors (Doshas) — Vata (air), Pitta (fire) and Kapha (water). These three most powerful forces in the macrocosm are also the main structuring forces in the microcosm (body). The three humors appear as the different constitutional types. Ayurveda sees individuals as generally predominant in one of these three humors.

Books on Ayurveda give a detailed examination of these humors, their variations and combinations. It is not necessary to understand one's predominant humor to practice Yoga, though it is helpful to know for general health purposes. The mental counterparts of the humors, however, are important for understanding the movement of the subtle energies that become activated through the process of Yoga.

The Subtle Doshas of Prana, Tejas, and Ojas

The three humors exist not only on a gross level, but also on a subtle level. The subtle or mental essences of the three biological humors of Vata, Pitta and Kapha are called Prana, Tejas and Ojas. As these are technical terms we cannot give them any simple English equivalents, other than correlating them to the spiritual energies of the elements. We can define them as follows:

> 1. Prana — which means the life-force or breath — like Vata, is the energy of air, but in its subtle or mental form, the ability to move our thoughts and perceptions.

> 2. Tejas — which means fire or radiance — like Pitta, is the energy of fire or digestion, but in its subtle or mental form, as in the power to digest ideas or emotions.

> 3. Ojas — which means underlying strength — like Kapha, is the energy of water, but in its subtle or mental form, as the underlying fluid energy reserve for the entire psycho-physical being, our underlying capacity for patience and mental endurance.

We can call Prana, Tejas and Ojas the subtle or spiritual energies of the respective elements of air, fire and water. They are the elements in their sublimated form as imbued with the energy of consciousness; they are not the physical elements. They are closer to the subtle elements, which in the astral body have a vital and mental action, but are also a little different than these. We could relate them more specifically with the causal elements, the root energies behind our entire manifestation and all of creation, both form and formless. They contain the powers of the Tanmatras or root sensory potentials.

Prana, Tejas and Ojas are ultimately the manifest reflection of the Absolute in its threefold nature as Being-Consciousness-Bliss (Sat-Cit-Ananda). Prana derives from Sat or pure Being as the will to live forever and to experience the fullness of life, which is to be one with all life. Tejas derives from Cit or pure consciousness as the will to know the truth, to have absolute knowledge, which is to know all the universe within oneself. Ojas derives from Ananda or pure bliss as the will to be eternally and perfectly happy, which is to find fulfillment in all things.

1. Being	Prana or Air	Life
2. Consciousness	Tejas or Fire	Light
3. Bliss	Ojas or Water	Love

The Divine principle of Sat-Cit-Ananda is reflected into the individual soul as its threefold nature of life (Prana), light (Tejas), and love (Ojas). Sat, as Prana or the life-force, imparts animation to the vehicles of the soul, which without it are mere immobile masses of matter. Cit, as Tejas or the power of sentience, imparts consciousness to the vehicles of the soul, which without it are unconscious. Ananda, as Ojas or the power of feeling, imparts sensitivity to the vehicles of the soul, which without it are dull, unfeeling and devoid of beauty. These three principles have a practical application for the development of awareness.

According to the *Chandogya*, one of the oldest *Upanishads*, there are three primal constituents of the manifest universe. These are:

1. Food or earth	Anna
2. Water	Apas
3. Fire	Tejas

These in turn have three subtle counterparts:

1. The essence of food is mind	Manas
2. The essence of water is breath	Prana
3. The essence of fire is speech	Vak

These three also correspond to Ojas (mind), Prana (breath) and Tejas (speech).

1. Food and mind	Ojas
2. Water and breath	Prana
3. Fire and speech	Tejas

Ojas is the underlying fluid-essence, derived from food, which supports and stabilizes the mind, particularly the emotional nature. The reproductive fluid becomes Ojas, which becomes the substance of the mind.

Prana here relates to the chief or original Prana, as apart from its diversification in its bodily functions. Prana resides in the fluids we take in, which serve as a vehicle for it. We note that water contains Prana or life-energy. For this reason Ayurveda recommends that we use fresh or pure water that has been aerated (thus giving it Prana).

Speech has a fiery nature and relates to Tejas. The heat and light we take into the body, particularly our sensory impressions, allow us to express and articulate ourselves through speech.

Locations of the Subtle Doshas in the Body

Prana, Tejas and Ojas have their specific sites in the subtle body, from which their prime activity originates. Fire or Tejas dwells in Earth, the Root or Muladhara Chakra at the base of the spine. This chakra is the highest abode of speech, wherein dwells Para Vak, the supreme state of speech.

Prana dwells in the heart, the Anahata Chakra or center of unstruck sound, which is also the Air Chakra. Ojas dwells in the head or the Crown Chakra.

As the Root Chakra, the Heart and the Head, Tejas, Prana and Ojas govern the three main centers of the subtle body and are responsible for its equilibrium, and through it the functioning of the physical body.

Agni, Vayu and Soma

These same principles are explained in the older Vedic tradition as the three main Vedic deities Agni (fire), Vayu (wind) and Soma (nectar or the Moon). Agni as fire corresponds to Tejas. Vayu as air corresponds to Prana (also called Vata in the *Vedas*). Soma as water corresponds to Ojas.

Agni, Vayu, and Soma have the same correspondences as Tejas, Prana, and Ojas. Agni corresponds to speech (Vak), Vayu (Indra) is Prana, and Soma, called amrit or the immortal nectar, is the essence of the bodily fluids (particularly the reproductive fluid or Shukra), like Ojas. Soma in Vedic thought also refers to the mind (manas).

Yet Agni, Vayu, and Soma are subtler than Tejas, Prana, and Ojas and refer more specifically to these three principles as energized via yogic practices. Ojas sublimated becomes Soma, the nectar of immortality. Tejas concentrated becomes Agni, the power of truth perception. Prana universalized becomes Vayu or Indra, the energy of the cosmic being.

The Movement of Kundalini

These three powers of Prana, Tejas and Ojas (Vayu, Agni and Soma), when activated and integrated through yogic practice, bring about the liberation of our consciousness and the realization of the Self (Atman) and the Absolute (Brahman).

Agni or fire dwells at the base of the spine (the Earth chakra) in the form of the Kundalini Shakti or serpent power, which has a fiery nature. Agni is placed in a kunda or altar in the ground, which inwardly is this earth center. This root fire is like the pilot light on a stove that sustains all of our physical functions.

Kundalini, like Agni, is also the essence of speech. She is composed of the various letters of the Sanskrit alphabet, which are bija mantras or root sound-energy patterns. These letters are depicted as the garland around the neck of this Goddess.

Soma or water (also the Moon) dwells in the head as the immortal nectar, like rain in the clouds of heaven. As Kundalini or Agni rises through the Sushumna or central channel, Soma or nectar descends and falls. The rising fire melts the heavenly nectar and causes it to flow in drops. When the fire reaches the top of the head and Soma permeates the body through the base of the spine, Self-realization occurs. At this point Agni and Soma exchange places and merge into the heart.

Vayu or Prana is lightning or electrical energy (vidyut), which drives the ascent of Agni and the descent of Soma. Prana in the heart requires integration, which proceeds through the joint action of Agni and Soma, or Tejas and Ojas. The union of Agni and Soma integrates and transforms Prana, which becomes the energy of immortality rather than that of mere mortality. This is said to be the birth of the spiritual man or being of consciousness, the Vedic deity Indra.

MENTAL COMPONENTS OF SPEECH (VAK) AND BREATH (PRANA)

The mind or conditioned consciousness as a whole in Vedanta is called the "internal organ" (antahkarana) in Sanskrit. It has three main functions:

1. Sensate Mind (Manas)
2. Reason (Buddhi)
3. Feeling (Citta)

Sensate Mind: Manas

Manas is the lower mind connected with the senses, through which we receive impressions from the external world. Manas has a dual role as both a sense organ and an organ of action. Through it we are able to coordinate our sensory and motor organs, like the eyes and hands, which otherwise would remain unconnected. Manas is thus considered to be the sixth sense organ. It is our means of action and expression in the external world.

Manas in common terms is the sensate mind, which is dominated by emotions, like desire, fear, and anger that allow us to respond in a personal way to stimuli from the external world. It is the site of our likes and dislikes and personal opinions about things. In the unevolved state the sensate mind causes us to come under the influence of the external world. In the evolved state it allows us to respond in a conscious and creative manner to external influences. Developing Manas through cultivating will, faith and desirelessness develops Ojas.

Feeling: Citta

Prana relates to Citta, which is the deeper sensitivity that underlies all mental functions. Just as Prana as the primary life-force is the foremost of the three factors of Prana, Tejas and Ojas, so Citta is the underlying field of conditioned consciousness, in which the impressions and memories of different births are stored. Citta is called the heart and dwells in the heart.

Citta is the general sensitivity of the mind which allows us to feel and to know things. Its purpose is to enable us to relate to things and to unite with the objects of our experience. It is not a reactive mechanism (like Manas), and functions independently of the senses. Whereas emotion through Manas is a response to an external stimuli, feeling via Citta is a state of mind independent of them. In this regard we could say that temporary emotional reactions come through Manas, but deep emotional states or deep feelings belong to Citta, including the craving for life that keeps us bound to the cycle of rebirth.

Reason: Buddhi

Tejas relates to Buddhi, the discriminating faculty, which has a fiery nature. Buddhi allows us to judge the reality of things — to discern truth from falsehood, or actuality from imagination. Buddhi is the basis of rationality, which can be directed toward the objects of the senses or toward the Divine or inner Self. Attached to the senses it discriminates the names, forms and numbers of the external world. It functions in a quantitative manner to create a materialistic idea of reality. Directed inward, Buddhi discriminates eternal truth from transient appearance, allowing us to negate the outer world into the reality of consciousness.

Unlike Manas, Buddhi functions independently of the senses, and is able to control them. Because of its capacity for decisive perception, Buddhi has a power of spiritual transformation which Manas and Citta can rarely bring about.

Citta, Buddhi and Manas have their functions in the subtle as well as the gross body. Citta and Buddhi exist also in the causal body, but not Manas since the causal body transcends all sensory functions on which

Manas is based. These higher functions of the mind can only be known through spiritual practice. There are two additional factors in the mind.

Ego (Ahamkara)
Individual Soul (Jivatman)

Ego is the power of identification, whereby we regard the body, or some other object or quality, as the Self. Ego is the factor of division and disease, both mentally and physically. The Jivatman or individual soul is our sense of being an eternal conscious being. It is the aspiration toward the Divine or truth that follows us from birth to birth. The Paramatman or supreme Self transcends all the functions of the mind. While the mind is composed of thoughts, the true Self is thought-free awareness. The Self is the real light which illumines the modifications of the mind and is never affected by them.

The three main components of the mind — Citta, Buddhi and Manas or feeling, reason and emotion — function between ego on one side and the Self on the other. Their action varies according to the direction in which they are oriented. Directed toward the Self they become awakened and their higher functions emerge. Directed toward the ego and the external world, their potential remains latent and they come into conflict with one another.

Citta or feeling is comparable to a chariot. The senses are the horses. Manas or the sense-oriented mind is the reins. The intelligence or Buddhi is the charioteer. The ego causes us to lose control of the horses and come under the influence of the external world. The Self gives us control of the horses and enables us to beyond all external influences.

EXAMINING PRANA, TEJAS AND OJAS

Prana, Tejas, and Ojas have various signs and symptoms within our psycho-physical complex through which we can monitor their condition. As the practice of Yoga generally increases all three, there is a danger that if one is increased more than the others, side effects may arise. To practice Yoga safely and successfully all three must be kept in a dynamic balance. It is possible for any of the three to fall into excess or deficient conditions temporarily. Many conditions which are regarded as meditational or Kundalini disorders are really imbalances of Prana, Tejas and Ojas. We should try to assess whether Prana, Tejas or Ojas are sufficient or whether their states are too high or too low. For this the following section has been divised.

SIGNS OF SUFFICIENT PRANA, TEJAS AND OJAS
Prana

Prana is sufficient when the breath is deep and full, when the body feels light and clean, when the limbs are supple and movement is easy, when the capacity to listen is well-developed, when there is much vitality, capacity for action, and when one has the ability to comprehend many different points of view.

Tejas

Tejas is sufficient when the body is able to endure cold, when the skin has luster, when the eyes are bright, when speech and perception are clear, the power of visualization is good, when right judgment and discrimination prevail, when the power of reason is high, and when one is self-reliant, courageous and free from delusions, expectations, emotional clinging and fear.

Ojas

Ojas is sufficient when the immune system is strong, when there is adequate energy in the reproductive system, when the mind and emotions are calm and steady, when one has endurance, stability, equanimity and fearlessness, and when there is faith, love, devotion, surrender, and patience.

SIGNS OF EXCESSIVE PRANA, TEJAS AND OJAS
Prana

Excess Prana causes loss of mental control and loss of sensory and motor coordination, with possible tremors or erratic movements. We feel spaced out, ungrounded, and may feel like we are losing our minds or sense of identity. Anxiety and palpitations may occur, along with insomnia, a general experience of disequilibrium or hyperventilation.

Tejas

Excess Tejas causes an overly critical and discriminating mind, with possible delirium, headache and burning sensation in the head and eyes. Clarity is excessive or destructive and we may become trapped in doubt or negativity. Anger, irritability and enmity are possible. On the spiritual path, we can become manipulative, dominating, fault-finding with others, and may have delusions of our own power and knowledge along with paranoia.

Ojas

Excess Ojas causes heaviness and dullness in the mind, as well as too much self-contentment that causes us to be unwilling to change or grow. Generally, high Ojas is much less a problem than high Prana and Tejas, which are the main factors in mental disorders. High Prana (excess air) dries out Ojas and high Tejas (excess fire) burns it up. Excess states of Prana and Tejas thus appear together with low Ojas.

SIGNS OF DEFICIENT PRANA, TEJAS AND OJAS

Prana

When Prana is deficient the breath is shallow or rapid, the body feels heavy, we lack vitality and ability to work, and we are lethargic, apathetic, lazy, or sluggish. We lack in mental energy, enthusiasm and curiosity. Our life-force and healing energy is low and we allow no new energy into our lives. Our mind and senses become dull and without motivation. Our attitudes will be conservative and rigid and we will fall under the rule of the past.

Tejas

When Tejas is deficient the body is cold, the skin is pale, the eyes lack luster, speech and perception are cloudy or confused, judgment and discrimination are unclear, and one is irrational, gullible, or full of wrong imaginations. When Tejas is too low we lack in capacity to inquire or discern. We uncritically accept things and lose the power to learn from or digest our experiences. Mentally we become too passive and impressionable and often come under the domination of others.

Ojas

When Ojas is deficient the immune system is weak, the reproductive secretions are depleted, the mind and emotions are unstable, we are easily bothered by noises or lights, there is fear, anxiety, restlessness, and insomnia. When Ojas is low we lack in self-confidence, are unable to concentrate, have poor memory and lack in faith. There will be little consistency to our thoughts or balance to our emotions. Nervous exhaustion or mental breakdowns become possible.

TANTRIC DEITIES FOR PRANA, TEJAS, AND OJAS

The Ten Great Wisdom Forms of the Goddess relate to the three principles of Prana, Tejas and Ojas, and can be used as tools to develop them. The Tantric system relates all three principles to the Goddess because the Goddess is the Yoga Shakti or power whereby Yoga proceeds.

> PRANA is Kali who is also time, movement and transformation.
> TEJAS or the root fire is named Bhairavi owing to her fierce nature.
> OJAS or the subtle nectar is named Sundari owing to her blissful nature.

The movement of Tantric Yoga is between the two triple forms of the Mother: Tripura Bhairavi (the terror of the three worlds) who exists in the form of Kundalini in the Root Chakra (the supreme speech or Para Vak), and Tripura Sundari (the beauty of the three worlds), who exists as Soma in the Crown Chakra (the supreme power of consciousness or Para Shakti). Kali dwells in the heart, in the middle, allowing for their integration. These are three most important of the Ten Wisdom Goddesses. Their worship is another way to gain control of these three principles. The other forms of the Wisdom Goddesses relate to the processes of the subtle body as has been discussed in their location and function.

4
TANTRIC AND AYURVEDIC SECRETS
FOR THE PRACTICE OF YOGA

*Yoga does not exist in heaven above, in the earth or in
the nether world. Those proficient in Yoga declare that
Yoga is the unity of the individual and the supreme Self.*
— Devi Gita VII.2

In this chapter we will examine how to develop the subtle energies of
the mind from both a Tantric and Ayurvedic perspective, focusing on
Prana, Tejas and Ojas, the spiritual energies of the air, fire and water, the
inner counterparts of the biological humors of Vata, Pitta and Kapha. First
we will outline the main principles and practices for the yogic path which
are of universal application.

GENERAL REGIMEN FOR YOGA PRACTICE
Yoga is a practice aimed at opening up our higher consciousness. It
is not simply yogic postures or exercises, which are small and preliminary
part of the yogic system. Yoga thus requires a certain discipline of life and
thought. The discipline of Yoga, though it can be explained in much detail,
rests upon a few simple principles, of which three are primary.

Peace of Mind
The foremost factor to consider is that our practice of Yoga must be
based on a firm foundation of peace of mind. Such peace is not merely a
superficial state of ease or relaxation, or release from stress, but a deep
stillness of the mind and heart. Surrender to the Divine or the inner Self
is the basis of practice, not any willful personal effort, much less the
seeking of some preconceived result or experience. This state of peace
should extend to our relationships, work, and environment. Without peace
of mind, whatever else we may do, our practice will lack the stability to
come to fruition.

Moderation in Sexual Activity
If we do not have adequate energy our practice will either literally run
out of gas, or have negative side-effects. As the sexual energy is the

ultimate energy source in the body, its power is required to effect a real inner transformation. This does not necessarily require celibacy, but it does require restricting the amount of energy lost through sexual activity.

Vegetarian Diet

A sattvic or pure diet should be followed as purity of food leads to purity of mind. The food we take in builds up all the bodily tissues and ultimately the mind itself. If that food is heavy (like meat), or disturbing in its qualities (very salty or spicy), the mind will lack the subtlety or stability for yogic practice. The toxins created by dead or devitalized food can clog or block the subtle channels and agitate the nerves.

Sattvic food consists of a vegetarian diet, using fruit, vegetables, nuts, grains, and dairy products, along with mild sweet spices like ginger, cinnamon and cardamom. Food should preferably be organic, fresh or freshly cooked. Meat, fish and eggs should be avoided. Natural sugars are allowed but not in excess. Beans, except mung, should be taken only in moderation. Salty and sour articles should similarly be used in moderation.

AYURVEDIC HEALTH REGIMENS

Yogic practitioners can benefit by modifying their diet and life-style relative to their predominant biological humor according to Ayurveda, so as to avoid causing imbalances in the life-force.

These factors are explained in detail in books on Ayurveda. Those who do not know their constitution can follow the general guidelines of a sattvic diet. Diets per constitution are important if we are suffering from some disease ailment. Otherwise we can safely follow a sattvic diet.

More specifically, yogic practices are part of Rasayana (rejuvenation) therapy in Ayurveda. This generally follows Pañcha Karma (purification) therapy. Those interested in the topic further can examine Ayurvedic teachings on Rasayana (rejuvenation) and Kaya Kalpa (transforming the physical body).

THE RIGHT ATTITUDE

Along with these three primary principles, we need the right attitude in our practice, which is that of awakened Self-awareness. This is the clear recognition that in our true nature we are immortal, infinite, beyond the body, mind and senses, free of all emotional and mental perturbation, and untouched by all pain, sorrow and desire. Yogic practice is thus a methodology for being ourselves, returning to our true nature, and claiming our inherent mastery of all time, space, matter and energy. Self-realization is not something to be created or gained for the first time, but is a giving up of all that is superficial, extraneous, or inessential. We must recognize that it is beneath our Divine dignity as immortal consciousness to want anything, to be afraid of anything, or to be dominated by anything coming from the external world which is merely our shadow. Our practice is not a seeking to gain anything new but a reclaiming of our eternal birthright to be one with the Unlimited.

Alternatively, a devotional attitude is helpful. Such an attitude is founded on the understanding that we are immortal children of the Divine Father and Mother, that Yoga is the natural route of returning to our eternal home, and that our practice is supported by our Divine parents who are ever present guiding and helping us, assuming whatever forms and experiences are necessary in order to teach us.

Another essential attitude is that of non-violence (ahimsa), which consists of not wishing harm to any creatures, but wishing peace, happiness, and freedom from suffering for all. Attitudes of exclusivism or intolerance along the spiritual path are also subtle forms of violence, and result in unwholesome or illusory experiences.

SPECIFIC REGIMENS FOR THE PRACTICE OF YOGA
Balancing The Subtle Doshas

As the forces of Yoga begin to awaken, we must learn how to develop them properly. In the following discussion of how to develop each of the three factors of Prana, Tejas and Ojas, some overlap of information occurs because these factors are interrelated. One should examine the information on all three to ensure their integral development. While information is given on matters ranging from diet and herbs to yogic approaches, the meditational practices are the most important.

Tejas is the central factor in the development of higher consciousness and the awakening of the Kundalini. It is the sacred fire, Agni, through which the yogic ritual proceeds. Hence we begin with Tejas.

5
HOW TO DEVELOP TEJAS
The Spiritual Energy of Fire

Divine Sun, nourisher, solitary seer, death who control
the power of creation, remove your rays and gather up
your radiance (Tejas), that I may perceive your most
auspicious form. The being in the Sun beyond, He am I!
— *Isha Upanishad 16*

TEJAS AND SPEECH

Tejas is the essence of speech, which has a fiery nature. Clear speaking thus increases fire or Tejas. Confused talk disperses Tejas like smoke from a poorly lit fire, and shows that our fire of speech is not functioning properly. Hence if we want to examine our Tejas we should look at our capacity to speak and to articulate ourselves. This is why fire-dominant (Pitta) individuals are good speakers and orators. However, harsh or critical speech makes Tejas too high or agitates it. Speech should be clear and truthful but also sweet and gentle to develop Tejas properly. Perhaps the worst thing that weakens Tejas is gossip, which includes gossip about spiritual teachers, groups and their personal affairs.

We both take in and give out speech. The words we take in are the food for our Tejas, those we give out are our expression of Tejas. The words we take in are not merely what we hear but what we understand, what we are able to discern as truth with the intelligence (Buddhi). Hence we should make sure to understand all that we hear. Similarly we should make our actions correspond to our words. We should do what we say and say what we do, and do things when and how we say we will. This power of truthfulness increases Tejas.

TEJAS AND WILL

Fire moves upward. The ascending fire represents our own individual striving for truth. Hence Tejas relates to the energy of will, volition and aspiration (Udana Vayu), which are also functions of the Buddhi. To increase our power of aspiration, our seeking of Divine truth, is another important impetus to Tejas.

Ganesha is the lord of wisdom and accomplishment who removes all obstacles. He should be invoked at the beginning of all important ventures, or whenever we encounter any obstructions. His mantra is:

Om gam gaṇeśāya namaḥ!

We should strive to ascend in life, to follow our higher impulses and forego the lower. We should sacrifice our lower drives into our ascending flame of aspiration. This is a kind of motivation but unlike the willful or self-aggrandizing drives of the ego. It is not a seeking of something for ourselves but the will to go beyond our personal limitations.

YOGIC PRACTICES
Mantra

Perhaps the main method of increasing Tejas is the chanting of mantras. Mantra increases Tejas and Vak (speech), and ultimately awakens the Goddess Kundalini, who is the essence of sound and mantra. For developing Tejas the mantra Hrīm (the main mantra of the Goddess) is important. It does not have special restrictions as to its usage.

The mantra Hūm is very useful as well, and actually stronger than Hrīm, though not quite as balanced in its effect. Hūm is very fiery — a mantra of Divine wrath, relating both to Shiva and to fire (Agni) — and therefore should not be used carelessly. Hūm can be used for invoking fire or stimulating Tejas. Svāhā can be used for offering any mantras into the sacred fire or Tejas. The mantra Dūm, the mantra of invincible Durga which takes us across all difficulties, can be used as well. The mantra Om itself is quite effective for Tejas as it is the sound of the Sun, though it is also good for Prana and Ojas. Om causes our energies to ascend and helps the Kundalini rise.

The most important mantra for creating Vak-shakti or the power of speech is the Panchadasi mantra, the fifteenfold syllable mantra of Sundari (note her section). This mantra, however, is also useful for Ojas and Prana, as it is very balanced. Another very balanced and generally useful mantra is the Vedic Gayatri, which is traditionally chanted at the rising and setting of the Sun, while enkindling the sacred fire or sitting facing the Sun.

However, if Tejas is too high, if our spiritual practice creates too much heat, light or burning sensations, we can use cooling and calming mantras like Mā or Aim.

The Practice of Silence

Mantra is a form of concentrated speech. It functions best if we reduce ordinary or dispersed forms of talking. The foundation for mantra is silence, which is another way to increase Tejas. Not speaking allows the energy of Tejas to increase and cuts off its outflow. However, in order to work it must be a real silence of mind, not merely a suppression of the vocal organ. The internal dialogue, which goes on unceasingly in the mind, must come to an end. This requires that we shift the focus of the mind to mantra, rather than thinking about problems and plans.

Deities

The Wisdom of Bhairavi is most important for developing Tejas (note her section). Her mantras are particularly strong, though not as commonly used as Hrīm and Hūm. The Wisdom of Tara and Chhinnamasta can be useful as well. Chhinnamasta is the great Goddess of discriminating perception, which is the highest action of Tejas. Otherwise the Goddess Durga, who rides the fiery lion, is specific to Tejas.

Besides the forms of the Goddess, Skanda, the son of Shiva and Parvati, relates specifically to Tejas. He wields the spear (shakti), destroys the demon of death (Tarakasura), and relates to the fiery planet Mars. In terms of the human body he represents the sexual fluid turned inward by the power of meditation. Rudra, the wrathful form of Shiva, also has a Tejas energy, as propitiated in the famous Rudram chant of the *Yajur Veda*. Agni, the Vedic deity for fire, has a similar nature and Vedic mantras to him help increase Tejas.

Meditational Methods

Discrimination (viveka) and inquiry (vichara) are the main meditational principles for developing Tejas, as they help develop the Buddhi, the fiery perceptive part of the mind. Discrimination and inquiry are the prime methods of the Yoga of Knowledge or Jñana Yoga, which is Tejas-predominant.

Discrimination consists of discerning between reality and unreality, truth and falsehood, the Self and the not-Self, the pure and the impure. Normally the Buddhi or discriminating principle is concerned with differentiating the names and forms of the outer world, measuring, pricing and naming things, creating various levels of worth, status or prestige. In this process the mind becomes caught in opinions, beliefs and judgments which attach it to the outer forms of things.

To develop Tejas we must turn the Buddhi around or reverse its ordinary and conditioned function. We must distinguish consciousness, which is the eternal formless subjective principle, from name and form, which are transient objective principles. We must focus on the presence of the object — which is not separate from the presence of the seer — and not allow our minds to dwell on the outer aspects of the object and its changing appearances. We must look directly at things without the veil of opinions, judgments, likes and dislikes of the conditioned mind. This is to dwell on the quality of things as apart from the quantities that we use to measure them. It is to commune with the presence of the object — to dwell in perception itself — and forget our ideas about it. In this way we discover a reality in all things that transcends their mere appearance or utility relative to our point of view.

Inquiry means entering into the source of our thoughts by tracing the I-thought back to its origin in the Self or pure consciousness (a method well explained by the modern sage Ramana Maharshi). For this we must learn to observe the thought current. We notice that all of our thoughts are based on the I-thought; the idea of the self is the basic reference point for all mental activities. However, the I-thought is composed of two factors, the I or subject, and the object with which we have identified ourselves. This takes many forms like "I am this," "I am that," or "this is mine." Our minds are filled with opinions and judgments like "I am happy or sad," "I am intelligent or unintelligent," "I am a success or a failure," "I am good or bad," "I am beautiful or ugly," "I am an American, a Christian, a Hindu," and so on.

We impose upon the Self various identities, mental or emotional qualities, physical conditions, levels of social status, or possessions and attachments. All of these go back to our basic self-image or I-am-the-body idea, which is the root of all attempts to externalize, materialize, or identify our Self. The true I or the I-in-itself cannot be known to us as long as we are pursuing such identifications. The true I is pure consciousness that transcends all qualities, quantities, and conditions. Inquiry consists of tracing out the pure I as distinct from the changing circumstances of the various identifications we have created around ourselves. This requires discrimination.

Passive meditation or mere mindfulness is not as effective in increasing Tejas. Mindfulness is usually better for developing Prana (Citta).

Other Yogic Techniques

Trataka or steady gazing at light sources, particularly ghee lamps (a cotton wick burning in ghee or clarified butter), also aids in the development of Tejas, but on a more outward level. Focusing on the outer light helps develop our inner light. We can focus upon the inner light directly. In the practice of Yoga various lights may come forth, particularly from the third eye. To meditate upon the inner light is another important yogic technique for Tejas.

Visualization practices using color similarly increase Tejas, particularly using bright colors like gold, orange, and red. Saffron orange is perhaps the best color for Tejas. These colors are used relative to deities like Bhairavi, Chandi or Durga, who have a fiery energy.

Types of Pranayama which use rapid deep breathing, like Bhastrika or Kapalabhati, increase fire and heat or Tejas, though they require some caution in their application. Generally anything that aids in the awakening of Kundalini helps develop Tejas, as Kundalini is primarily Tejas.

Ritual fire offerings, Vedic practices like Homa and Agnihotra, are the best outer practices. But in these it is important to reflect upon the outer fire as a counterpart for our inner fire and to learn to offer our thoughts and feelings into this inner fire, Tejas, the radiance of the Self.

HERBS AND DIET

Certain foods and herbs can be helpful for Tejas, but this is a secondary consideration. The most useful herb for Tejas is calamus (Acorus calamus), whose Sanskrit name Vacha means speech. Similar fiery herbs (usually pungent in taste) are useful, like tulsi (holy basil), bayberry, sage, pippali, and camphor (in small amounts like 250 mg). These herbs as aromas or incense are also useful. Heena (henna) or camphor as incense are specific in this regard.

Spices are useful along with the diet, particularly those of a sattvic nature (ginger, cinnamon, coriander, cardamom, fennel, basil, turmeric, saffron). A light heat-increasing diet is best, including seeds and nuts like sesame and almond, and grains like wheat. Honey helps Tejas and can be taken with Tejas-increasing herbs and foods.

Special Ayurvedic mercury preparations aid in increasing Tejas. According to Tantric thought, mercury is the semen of Lord Shiva (the masculine principle) and has a fiery or Tejas-predominant nature. Sulfur also has a Tejas quality and corresponds to the menstrual fluid of the Goddess. These two, prepared and rendered non-toxic through special Ayurvedic practices, are helpful for developing Tejas. Most specific is the Ayurvedic compound Makaradhwaj. This formula, however, is very powerful and should be taken seasonally (late fall or winter) and generally only for short periods of time.

Important for increasing Tejas is fasting, particularly allied with mantra and meditation. Fasting allows the inner fire to increase and to burn up impurities in the body. Yet for long term fasting not to have negative side-effects we must have sufficient Ojas to begin with. Taking spice teas like ginger, cinnamon or calamus during fasting aids additionally in increasing Tejas.

On the other hand, ghee and raw sugar help moderate the effects of too much heat (or too much chanting), without depressing Tejas. Ghee is specific for developing Tejas in a harmonious manner. Herbs like gotu kola (brahmi and mandukaparni) also keep Tejas from getting too high.

The use of coconut oil externally (particularly Brahmi Oil, or gotu kola prepared in a coconut oil base) will also allay high Tejas. Flower oils and fragrances, like rose, jasmine and saffron, are helpful in reducing high Tejas, as well as sandalwood oil and khus (vetivert). On the other hand, sesame or almond oils applied externally help increase Tejas, as do most aromatic oils like eucalyptus, cedar or wintergreen.

GEMS

According to Vedic mythology, the fiery planet Mars is born from the Earth and so corresponds with Tejas, which arises from the Earth Chakra. Red coral, the Vedic gemstone for Mars, is good for developing Tejas.

The Sun is even hotter and more fiery than Mars. Ruby (or its substitute garnet), the gemstone for the Sun, also increases Tejas. Ketu, the dragon's tail or south node of the Moon, has a fiery nature in the Vedic system. Its gem, cat's eye (chrysoberyl), is perhaps the strongest gemstone for increasing Tejas, as it relates to the energy of fire on a psychic or astral level as the power of subtle perception. Gold as a metal generally increases Tejas. Gems for the Sun or Mars are best worn on the Sun finger (right ring finger). However, they can also be worn on the Jupiter finger (index finger).

Such astrological measures are best advised relative to the birth chart, particularly regarding the more expensive stones. For this one should consult a qualified Vedic astrologer. We note that few yogis wear gems. This may not be merely because they cannot afford to. Mantric and meditational methods are more direct and powerful for influencing the subtle body and mind than are material substances like gems. However helpful, gems are not essential to the yogic process.

Gems can be taken internally in the form of special preparations. Ayurvedic medicine contains specially prepared gem oxides called bhasmas, which can be used for this purpose. Gold oxide ash can be used for Tejas. Coral oxide ash (Praval Bhasma), can be used, or another less expensive coral preparation (Praval Pishti). Ruby oxide ash (Manikya Bhasma) is useful but very expensive. Such minerals are taken in small dosages according to Ayurvedic instruction.

In addition, tinctures of gems can be taken internally, either using water or alcohol as the medium of extraction. For water extractions the gemstone, either in its uncut or cut form, is soaked in water over night, along with a small amount of a nervine herb like tulsi (holy basil), calamus, or gotu kola, which aid in extracting the subtle essence of the gem. For alcoholic tinctures a solution of 50% alcohol and 50% water can be used, leaving the gem to soak for a week or longer. Ten to twenty drops of the alcohol tincture, or a teaspoon of the water tincture can be taken daily to give a mild support for Tejas.

Similarly, homeopathic forms of gems can be used. They are quite safe and usually stronger than the tinctures. Various mantras can be used to empower such gem remedies, including those for the planets that rule the gems, or those for the deities relating to the qualities that we are seeking to develop through them.

6
HOW TO DEVELOP PRANA
The Spiritual Energy of Air

Indra speaks: I am Prana, the Self of intelligence.
Worship me as the immortal life.
— *Kaushitaki Upanishad* III.2

YOGIC PRACTICES
Pranayama: Breathing Exercises

Prana as breath is increased mainly through the practice of Pranayama, most specifically through the prolonged natural retention of breath. This is aided by keeping the body and senses still, which requires the practice of Yoga postures (asana) and control of the senses (pratyahara). As long as the body is agitated or contains accumulated stress in the muscles and joints, the Prana cannot move freely. As long as the mind follows the impulses of the senses, our breath and vitality must remain agitated. Hence we must learn to relax the body and to control the senses. Control of the senses does not mean suppressing sensory impulses but, rather, not letting ourselves be dominated by the senses. The senses are only our instruments and, like our horses, should not be telling us where to go.

The best time to gather Prana is one or two hours before Dawn, the so-called hour of Brahman (Brahma muhurta), when Prana is most available to the psyche. The times of sunrise, noon and sunset are also useful, as at these transitional moments the movement of Prana can be changed in a significant way. The time immediately before sleep helps release the Prana through the dream state and open up the astral and causal energies.

We must learn to consciously direct the energy of the breath. This is helped by understanding the five Pranas and their different movements (note section). This can be aided by visualizing the activities and the movements of Prana through the different channels and chakras. Most important is directing the energy of the breath up the spine during inhalation and down the spine during exhalation. Keeping the Prana in the spine calms the mind, centralizes our energy, and facilitates peace of mind.

Being able to stop the Prana at will is the highest goal but should never be forced. It cannot be accomplished by personal effort, which merely adds tension and therefore keeps the life-force disturbed, but only by a deep relaxation and letting go. One should begin with prolonged deep breathing and only gradually develop prolonged retention as it comes of itself. For this So'ham Pranayama is the most natural. Mentally repeat the mantra "So" on inhalation and the mantra "Ham" on exhalation and simply allow the breath to gradually calm itself. Merely counting the breath has a soothing effect, but the use of mantra adds more energy and is stronger because it links the mind with the breath. Mantra along with the breath can be directed towards the Deity to give the additional energy of devotion; or it can be linked with a process of meditative inquiry to give the power of insight.

Although Pranayama generally increases Prana, right nostril (solar breathing) increase Tejas and left nostril (lunar breathing) increases Ojas. Hence Pranayama can be used for developing Prana, Tejas or Ojas depending on how it is performed.

Exhalation should generally last twice as long as inhalation. Retention of the breath should first be done after exhalation and should initially be made to last as long as inhalation. Eventually it can be practiced after both inhalation and exhalation, and be of the same length as exhalation. In this way one can come to have one full breath last a minute or longer. Alternate nostril breathing, like drawing water with a straw, gives greater control over the breath, and is the preferable method to subdue the Prana. The use of the yogic locks or bandhas (Mula, Jalandhara, Uddiyana) can aid in the stabilization of Prana.

As Pranayama can be dangerous, both caution and guidance are necessary. When thought begins to subside and our life-energy is directed inward the breath naturally comes to rest. This is what we should seek rather than artificially trying stop the breath, which may only deprive us of the necessary oxygen for the blood.

There are additional Pranayama methods in which we gather in the life-force from the natural world through our senses. They require being in a natural environment and allowing one's life-force to expand into the whole of Nature. One can stand in an open area and visualize the life-force from Nature coming into oneself during inhalation, while during exhalation visualizing one's life-force permeating all of Nature. One should concentrate on absorbing Prana through all the senses but particularly through the eyes. For this process it helps to have the arms extended upon inhalation, and closed on exhalation.

A method of Pranayama relating to the Yoga of Knowledge is negate the external world upon exhalation and affirm one's reality as pure consciousness upon inhalation. There are many Pranayama techniques, most particularly the Kriya Yoga techniques of the Yoga tradition of Lahiri Mahashaya, brought to the West by Paramahansa Yogananda. These help develop Prana but can aid in Tejas and Ojas depending upon their specific forms and how we apply them.

Mantras

While mantra is specifically for Tejas, many mantras are useful for Prana, like the Kali mantra Krīm, or the Sarasvati mantra Aim. Kali increases the Pranic force generally. She aids in separating the Prana from its identification with the physical body. She helps us accomplish work that is beyond our ordinary capacity. Sarasvati increases our intellectual functions, including a broader creativity and comprehension, as opposed to the direct and concentrated but sometimes narrow perception of Tejas.

When our Prana is too agitated or disturbed in its movement, calming mantras like Mā, Shānti or Rām can be used. They help settle and ground the Prana and restore its equilibrium.

Deities

Stopping the Prana is one of the fruits of the worship of Bagala. General control of Prana comes through the worship of Kali. Bhuvaneshvari is useful for giving space in which to allow our life-force to expand. Dhumavati is useful for connecting us with the source of life which transcends manifestation. However, she can cause us to lose contact with the life-force manifest in our present incarnation.

For giving mastery over the Prana, the deity Hanuman (the monkey God and companion of the avatar Rama) is perhaps the most important. He is said to have been born of the wind God (Vayu), but he is also regarded as a portion of Lord Shiva. Among Vedic deities Indra is most specific to Prana. Vedic mantras to Indra can be chanted to increase Prana. Lord Shiva himself relates to Prana, but to the fiery or Tejas aspect of it (as Rudra).

Meditational Approaches

Passive and receptive forms of meditation — emphasizing space, infinity and openness — increase Prana. Meditating on the sky is a simple method. For this one should lie down flat in an open area outdoors, preferably on a cloudless day, and gaze at the sky (though keeping the eyes away from the sun). This should be done for fifteen to thirty minutes, which is usually enough time to allow the cosmic Prana to be absorbed. One can also do this practice at night. It is best to start after sunset but before dark and gaze at the sky until all the stars come out. This will connect us with cosmic space and give us a sense of Prana. It also helps reduce Tejas and improves the power of vision.

Another method is to focus on the space between things rather than objects themselves. For example, one can try to discern the space between the leaves of a tree, rather than focusing on the actual leaves. One thereby learns to see space as the reality rather than merely to see objects as real in themselves. In this way the space-like nature of all objects will become evident.

Meditation upon the void is another way. For this one must contact the voidness within the mind, as the mind after all has no particular shape, form or location. Externally one can visualize all things, particularly one's body, as empty. We can meditate upon the infinite space of the void as dwelling in our own hearts, in which the entire universe is contained.

Wherever space is created there must come into being a force or Prana to move within it. The key to creating energy is to create space. Once the right space is created, the energy or spirit must come forth of its own accord. Similarly, energy is mastered by creating a space of consciousness, by creating the proper environment for the energy, not by trying to control the energy directly, which only causes greater constriction. All of us should maintain a special sacred space in our house, like an altar or meditation room, for this purpose. Similarly we should visualize a sacred space as existing around us. Actually all space is sacred and the sacred is of the nature of space.

Another meditative method is the simple practice of mindfulness. In this we are simply aware of things as they are, rather than thinking about or reacting to them. We should constantly return the mind to the presence of some actual object and restrain its tendency to become caught in imagination or internal conversation. This can be done in Nature, using the objects of the natural world like mountains, rocks, trees or clouds. Such a practice of presence develops space and Prana. In this way Citta, the mental component of Prana, which is the receptive awareness of the heart, can be developed. Buddhist Vipassana meditation is of this type. One of the best objects to focus on for such mindfulness practice is the breath itself.

The Role of Sound and Music: Nada

Prana is a sound vibration, nada, that exists within space. Listening to uplifting music is an ordinary way to increase Prana. Creating our own music is yet stronger, providing it is attuned to the vibration of consciousness. Indian ragas, as they are not limited to a rigid pattern, have a special effect for deconditioning the mind and aligning the nervous system with the cosmic life-force.

We can similarly listen to the inner unplayed music, the nada or inner sounds. For this we have to close the ears and listen within, particularly at the right ear. Various sounds arise in the process of internal listening like those of a drum, bell, shell, or flute. To follow these sounds is an important yogic method used in many traditions (like Laya Yoga and Surat Shabda Yoga).

While colors are more specific to Tejas, some colors are useful for Prana. Most important is deep or dark blue (nila), the color of infinite space (and is the color of Hindu deities like Shiva, Vishnu, Rama, Krishna and Kali). Also helpful is the color green, particularly emerald green, the color of the life-force on earth.

HERBS AND DIET

These are a secondary concern for developing Prana but can be helpful. The most useful herb for Prana and Citta is brahmi (gotu kola) or its equivalent mandukaparni, but other bitter herbs can be helpful. The use of the Ayurvedic formula Triphala, composed of the three herbs haritaki, amalaki and bibhitaki, insures the right absorption of Prana from food (which, according to Ayurveda, occurs in the large intestine). Mild spices like coriander, mint, parsley and cilantro are also useful.

A light, Vata-increasing (and Kapha-reducing) diet is helpful, as long as adequate fluids are taken in. For this raw food, greens, sprouts, and vegetable juices are good. Light aromatic oils like khus (vetivert), mint, wintergreen, or eucalyptus help develop Prana. Fasting can be used to increase Prana, but it should be combined with green juices (like celery, spinach, or cilantro; or wheatgrass, sunflower and alfalfa sprouts for a stronger effect), or astringent and cooling herb teas, like gotu kola, burdock, or dandelion. The use of regular tea in moderation helps clear the mind and facilitate Prana.

As water keeps Prana in equilibrium, care must be taken whenever Prana is being developed to keep the body hydrated properly, with fresh spring water (exposed to air and sunlight) or rain water being best, particularly when taken with lime, salt and sugar. When Prana is too high demulcent foods like milk, ghee, nuts and raw sugar, or demulcent herbs like shatavari, comfrey root, or licorice should be used. Oil massage with sesame oil — particularly to the head, neck, back or feet — is excellent for keeping Prana in balance when it becomes too high.

GEMS

Prana is governed primarily by the planet Saturn. Gemstones for Saturn like blue sapphire, lapis lazuli, or amethyst aid in the development of Prana. Gems for Mercury like emerald, green zircon, green tourmaline, or peridot are also useful. The better quality of these gemstones can be set in gold, the others in silver. Gems for Saturn are best worn on the Saturn finger (middle finger). Those for Mercury can be worn on the Mercury finger (little finger) as well as the Saturn finger.

Relative to gem preparations the oxide ash of emerald is available in Ayurvedic medicine (Markanda Bhasma). Water extracts, alcohol tinctures, or homeopathic preprations of these gems can also be used.

7
HOW TO DEVELOP OJAS
The Spiritual Energy of Water

Then his Ojas shone brilliantly, when Indra rolled up
both Heaven and Earth as if in a skin (the human body).
— *Rig Veda VIII.6.5*

Ojas as the material component among the three subtle Doshas is mainly increased through right diet, Ojas-increasing herbs, and preservation of the sexual energy. It cannot be simply increased on a mental level alone, but requires the intake of certain nutrients. However, yogic and meditational practices are helpful not only for developing but for transforming Ojas and uniting it with Tejas and Prana.

YOGIC PRACTICES
Bhakti Yoga

Attitudes like peace, faith, devotion, and equanimity are important in the development of Ojas. Generally all true virtues like modesty, compassion and love work directly to increase Ojas. Patience is perhaps the key word for developing Ojas. Perseverance and endurance, which requires time and consistency, are also useful qualities to develop Ojas. Ojas comes to us in little drops (called bindus) that fall into our consciousness. We must have a vessel to gather and store them. This requires an ongoing receptivity of mind. Feminine qualities of surrender and openness are helpful.

The ability to concentrate (dharana) the mind is important as this allows Ojas to be concentrated. For this meditation on a form, particularly that of a deity or guru, can be very helpful. Whatever works to stabilize the mind aids in developing Ojas, particularly controlling the emotions. For this we should not allow the mind to be dominated by the senses, but center it in the heart, in the contentment of our deeper nature. We should surrender our emotions, particularly desire and attachment, which cause Ojas to be dispersed. The state of emptiness behind desire drains Ojas. To counter this we should cultivate the feeling of fullness (Purna), that all is infinite, perfect and pure.

For Ojas all the methods of the Yoga of Devotion (Bhakti Yoga) are indicated, as it is Ojas-predominant. These include ritual worship (puja), communion with the deity, visualization of the deity as dwelling within the heart, and songs or chants to the deity (kirtana). To constantly engage one's heart and mind in service to the Divine connects us with the immortal power.

Karma Yoga, the Yoga of service (seva), is also helpful for Ojas. To put ourselves into the role of a servant of Divine grace links us up to the power of Ojas. Selfless service gathers our energy and causes outer attachments to fade. It gives us the strength of cosmic Ojas and the power of alignment in action with the Divine Will.

Mantra

Mantras like Om or Rām (the name Rama) aid in the development of Ojas. OM increases our energy generally. Rām has a protective and fortifying action. The mantra Shrīm is useful, as it is the mantra of the Goddess Lakshmi, who possesses a watery nature, and gives love, beauty and fertility. The mantra Mā along with meditation on the Divine Mother is very useful. Such mantras must be repeated with faith and attention and regularly for long periods of time. For developing Ojas the devotional quality is more important than the actual mantra itself.

Deities

Among the Ten Wisdom Goddesses, Kamala is important for increasing Ojas, as she increases devotion and Soma (nectar). Hence Lakshmi, the consort of Vishnu, of whom Kamala is an aspect, is also good. Sundari is important because she allows Soma to flow down from the Crown chakra. Bagala helps by stopping the restless movement of Prana, which allows Ojas to increase. The Divine Mother in all her forms helps promote Ojas because she is the ultimate resort of the water energy of the universe and the supreme ground of all nourishment and care.

Lord Vishnu, the preserver of the universe, a deity of water, is similarly helpful, particularly in his form of Narayana, the cosmic man who reclines on the cosmic sea. In this regard, the avatars of Vishnu help increase Ojas. Krishna is perhaps most important as he represents the energy of Divine love and bliss. The Hare Krṣna mantra (Hare Krṣna Hare Krṣna! Krṣna Krṣna Hare Hare! Hare Rāma Hare Rāma! Rāma Rāma Hare Hare!) is helpful, as is the great mantra for Vishnu Om Namo Bhagavate Vāsudevāya. These increase the love aspect of Ojas.

Even Lord Shiva, though he is the destroyer of the universe, increases Ojas by his power to give us peace and by his rulership over the Moon (the mind). His mantra — Om Namaḥ Shivāya — is very calming and can be used for increasing the peace aspect of Ojas. Ganesha, the first son of Lord Shiva and Parvati, is important for Ojas. Having the head of an elephant, he symbolizes strength, the ability to overcome obstacles, and an uninterrupted development of energy.

Brahmacharya: Control of Sexual Energy

Perhaps the main practice for increasing Ojas is Brahmacharya (control of sexual energy). This is why Brahmacharya has always been such an important principle in the practice of Yoga. Ojas is the ultimate product of nutrition that ends with the production of the reproductive tissue. Preservation of the sexual fluid not only helps with Ojas, it also helps with Tejas, which the reproductive fluid nurtures, and serves to ground the Prana so that it does not get agitated or disturbed.

Yet conservation of the sexual fluid should be combined with yogic practices like Pranayama, mantra and meditation to allow the Ojas to be used properly. Otherwise the unused energy will stagnate and cause various physical and psychological problems. As the orgasm is the point in sexual activity where the most energy is lost, particularly for men, this should be reduced as much as possible. The seals and locks (bandhas) of Hatha Yoga practice aid in this.

HERBS AND DIET

Diet is very important for developing Ojas because Ojas is the essence of food. Ojas-increasing food is indicated like dairy products, particularly milk and ghee (clarified butter). Milk should preferably be raw and taken from cows who have been treated humanely, which is seldom the case in commercial dairies. It should be drunk after being heated to the boiling point, with the addition of spices like cardamom or ginger and some natural sweetener. Ghee should preferably be made from raw milk. Natural sugars, like dried sugar cane juice or maple syrup, are good for developing Ojas, as is fresh honey (less than six months old). Seeds and nuts are important, particularly almond and sesame (the black seeds are best). Whole grains are helpful, particularly wheat and basmati rice. Most beans are not useful, except mung or urad dhal. Root vegetables are helpful, particularly potatoes or jerusalem artichokes. Ghee and sesame oil are perhaps the two most important items. Fruit is generally helpful as a secondary food, particularly grapes and dates.

Ojas-increasing herbs are indicated. These are the tonics and rasayanas (rejuvenatives) of Ayurvedic medicine like amalaki, ashwagandha, shatavari, lotus seed or root, shilajit, bala, vidari, licorice, and a combination of ten roots called Dashamula. These are best taken with raw sugar or fresh honey along with milk and ghee. The amalaki-based herbal jelly, Chyavan prash, is excellent (it also pacifies Tejas and Prana).

Similar Chinese herbs useful for Ojas are lycium berries, ginseng (either American or Chinese), dioscorea, dang gui, rehmannia, and he shou wu, herbs that are primarily tonics, particularly to the kidneys and reproductive systems.

Aphrodisiacs (vajikaranas) like garlic and onions, which can irritate the sexual organs, should not be used in significant amounts. Care must be taken with hot spices like cayenne, black pepper, or mustard because they tend to dry up Ojas. All food that is very heating in its properties, particularly meat, fish and shell fish, should be avoided. Meat and fish does not produce the pure form of Ojas needed for the practice of Yoga. Meat increases a lower grade of Ojas but also stimulates the body to discharge it.

Massage with oils, particularly sesame, helps increase Ojas and keep Prana in check. Sesame oil formulas like Mahanarayan Tail based on shatavari and ashwagandha, are yet stronger. Oil massage can be done once or twice a week before sleep, and is best followed by a shower.

Adequate deep sleep is necessary for developing Ojas. When Ojas is low a period of rest or deep peaceful meditation is necessary. The best sleep for increasing Ojas occurs between 10:00 P.M. and 4:00 A.M. Sleep after sunrise or during the day may cause stagnation in the body and will not help develop Ojas. On the contrary, it disturbs both mind and Prana.

GEMS

Ojas is related to the Moon (Soma), which represents our vital fluids. Gems for the Moon, the most important of which is pearl, help increase Ojas. Gems for Jupiter and Venus, which are both watery planets, can similarly be useful. Jupiter stones give strength in general and energize the immune system. Venus stones specifically increase sexual vitality. Jupiter gemstones include yellow sapphire, golden topaz, or citrine, while those for Venus are diamond, white sapphire, clear zircon, or quartz crystal. Gemstones for the Moon or Jupiter should be worn on the ring or index fingers. Those for Venus should be worn on the middle or little finger.

The Ayurvedic oxide ash of pearl (Moti Bhasma) helps increase Ojas. Diamond oxide ash (Hira Bhasma) is stronger, but is the most expensive and generally used only in extreme conditions. Coral ash (Praval Bhasma) can be used, though it will increase Tejas as well. Silver ash (Rajata Bhasma) and conch shell ash (Shankha Bhasma) are also useful. Water extractions or alcohol tinctures of these gems can be used, or homeopathic preparations of them, though their effect will be less strong.

PROTECTING OJAS

Ojas is depleted more easily than Tejas or Prana. We must protect our Ojas by not allowing energy to be lost by excessive physical, emotional, or mental activity. Emotional strain and agitation is the worst, particularly worry and anxiety. Disease, stress, excess travel, overwork (whether physically or mentally), or too much exercise can deplete Ojas. Exposure to the elements, to the wind and sun, particularly too much heat, noise or environmental pollution similarly depletes Ojas. Too much exposure to the mass media and excessive social contact are additional factors that can lower Ojas.

8
INTEGRAL DEVELOPMENT
OF PRANA, TEJAS AND OJAS:
Balancing the Spiritual Elements

While some Yoga practitioners may need to develop one of these three energies primarily, if one is particularly low, the usual procedure is to develop all three together. In the practice of Yoga all three factors are increased, sometimes rapidly. Hence it is important to take care to maintain the harmony and right proportion between each. Whenever one becomes higher than the others — even if the others are not necessarily low — difficulties or obstructions can arise. For this reason yogic practitioners have to be more mindful about diet, environment, impressions, and emotional reactions than ordinary people.

As Tejas is fire, we should increase it with discretion, never willfully or forcefully. However, for the spiritual life Tejas is usually the most important factor and so we should not ignore it. Without sufficient Tejas we lack the clarity and decisiveness to really accomplish anything.

As Prana is air, there is danger of ungroundedness or instability in its development, which can disrupt the basic equilibrium of the body and mind. Hence it also requires discretion in efforts to increase it. Ojas is the safest of the three to develop but, as latent energy, it alone is not sufficient to motivate us spiritually.

INTEGRAL PRACTICE

Prana, Tejas and Ojas support each other. Keeping the Prana up or in an ascending motion helps sustain Ojas, as the upmoving Prana prevents the loss of Ojas through downward discharges (Apana Vayu). This can be done by doing Pranayama exercises that keep the Prana in the spine. Tejas is also allied with the upward movement of Prana (Udana Vayu), and is increased along with it. Abundant Ojas naturally supports both Tejas and Prana, and provides an energy reserve for them to draw on. Tejas can aid in the energization of Ojas and the pacification of Prana.

It is best to develop Prana, Tejas, and Ojas together. Dietarily it is best to seek to develop Ojas, as Ojas requires a material support. Prana can be developed mainly through Pranayama. Tejas requires mantra and meditation. All three can be increased integrally during the same practice. For example, one can combine Pranayama (for Prana), mantra (for Tejas), and devotion (for Ojas), while following an Ojas-increasing diet. Or one can combine passive awareness meditations (for Citta-Prana) alternately with inquiry or discrimination practices (for Buddhi-Tejas), and faith and devotional practices (for Manas-Ojas). Such is the basis of most Yoga practices, particularly in Raja Yoga or the integral path.

The Union of Tejas and Ojas as Creating Prana

As Tejas (fire) and Ojas (water) unite they produce Prana (air). The unification of Tejas and Ojas creates a higher Pranic force. The rising fire of Tejas (the Mother) melts the nectar of Ojas (the Father), which descends, causing the Pranic being (the Child) to be born and grow. The integral development of Tejas and Ojas creates Prana of the highest order, in which no imbalances can occur.

This can be done by uniting mind (Manas, Father) and speech (Vak, Mother). Such a process occurs when we meditate upon mantra and contact its force and meaning. This gives rise to Prana (Citta, the child) as the realization or understanding of the mantra. Another method is to unite emotion (Manas) and reason (Buddhi). This occurs when we align our emotions to the power of discrimination and inquiry (viveka and vichara). We must use our attention with discernment to control the outward movements of emotion. Out of this arises consciousness (Citta), the mind-field cleared of its impressions, expanding into infinite space.

THE SOLAR YOGA

Everything can be accomplished through the Yoga of the Sun, which has an integral power. To meditate upon the inner Self as the spiritual Sun in the heart is the simplest method. The practice of submerging the mind in the spiritual heart (the inner Sun) functions to attune all the forces of our nature. Yoga in the highest sense is simply being who we really are. The inner energies of Prana, Tejas, and Ojas manifest naturally if we reside in the integrity and independence of our own nature. Yoga is really the easiest and most natural of all practices. Dangers associated with it occur only when we lose contact with our inner being and try to use the mind and ego to achieve results. The only real result we should seek in Yoga is to no longer seek anything.

MEDITATIONAL AND KUNDALINI DISORDERS

Yogic practices are part of a subtle science and technology to develop and harness latent higher powers behind the mind-body system. In Yoga, we are the laboratory. Our own psycho-physical complex is the site of the experiment. We cannot expect to develop the skills to use subtle yogic energies if we don't approach them with at least the same amount of patience and determination as a research scientist. Maturity of character, concentration of mind, and a great deal of consistency are necessary.

If one tries to develop Tejas or Prana without the proper Ojas to support them, many difficulties can occur. This is the cause of most so-called Kundalini and meditational disorders happening today. Such disorders usually involve derangements of Prana, Tejas and Ojas, not necessarily anything relative to the Kundalini itself, which is very seldom aroused accidentally.

Ojas is our capacity to hold higher energies. It is like the watt capacity of our light bulb (the mind). Tejas is like the power of the current going through the bulb, while Prana is the velocity of the current. If we increase Tejas and Prana but not Ojas, it is like trying to put a thousand watts into a hundred-watt light bulb. The bulb will merely burst. Hence most meditational disorders occur in people who have not developed Ojas properly. They have not developed the capacity to handle the strong energies they are trying to develop.

Unless we have controlled our sexual energy, unless our diet is pure and yet nutritive, unless we have faith, equanimity and devotion — in short unless Ojas is ripe — we do not have the foundation to properly undertake strong yogic practices like Pranayama, mantra and meditation, even if we can understand them conceptually. If we attempt such practices without this foundation we may arrive at certain experiences, but they are likely to be unwholesome, illusory or misleading. It is not enough for our intellects (Tejas) to be sharp. We must have an Ojas-supporting life-style as the right basis for practice.

So-called Kundalini disorders involve wrong movement of Prana, causing disturbed mental or neuro-muscular functioning, or premature development of Tejas, which burns up the mind and nervous system. Loss of equilibrium and irregularity in the digestive system is a derangement of Samana Vayu (the equalizing air). Uncontrolled movement of the limbs is a derangement of Vyana Vayu (the diffusive air). Uncontrolled speaking or coughing is a derangement of Udana Vayu (the ascending air). Hyper-sensitivity is usually a derangement of the Prana Vayu (the internalizing air). Problems with the urino-genital system reflect a derangement of Apana Vayu (the downward moving air).

Derangements of Tejas involve burning sensations, particularly to the head, sensitivity to light or bright colors, and unusual or extreme moods of irritability, anger or temper. Such derangements can generally be countered by developing Ojas, which, however, takes time and patience. They can be countered by the regimens for lowering high Tejas or Prana already discussed.

There are times when a low quality Ojas becomes excessive. This causes various mediumistic abilities characterized by overweight and an inability to control the mind, emotions and imagination. Such an overly passive nature can allow subtle forces and entities to work through it, but there is usually no real control over the process, which in turn can cause some damage to the equilibrium of body and mind. This usually arises from a lack of Tejas wherein perception and discrimination are weak.

Kundalini disorders may involve some portion of Kundalini energy going out into the peripheral nadis, rather than to the Sushumna or central channel. If some portion of the Kundalini energy enters the solar channel (Pingala Nadi), excess Pitta and Tejas is created, with excess heat and anger in the system causing pride and a domineering attitude. If it enters the lunar channe (Ida Nadi), excess Kapha and Ojas is created. The person may put on much weight along with developing psychic abilities that may be deranging, including unstable emotional states. If the Kundalini goes back and forth between these two nadis, Vata disorders can be created, with insomnia, hallucinations, fear and anxiety.

Individuals of Vata (air-predominant) and Pitta (fire-predominant) constitutions in particular may not have the proper Ojas to keep their practices stabilized, as constitutionally they tend to have less of it. They should scrutinize their Ojas carefully before embarking on any intense practices. Individuals of Kapha (water-predominant) constitution may have adequate Ojas but lack the clarity of Tejas and hence get trapped in inferior emotional or imaginative states. They should consider how to use their Ojas properly through increasing Tejas and Prana.

Meditational practices, however, are meant to take us out of our ordinary consciousness, to free us from the idea of the reality of the external world, and to dissolve the ego. These are often regarded as aberrations according to the standards of present society and its materialistic sciences. In the practice of meditation we may go through temporary imbalances as readjustment phases. Unusual Pranic movements, the experience of powerful emotions, seeing inner lights and hearing inner sounds, visions, contacting gurus and deities telepathically and so on, are not necessarily signs of disorders. Usually a new equilibrium will come after a short period of time.

Most meditational practices are safe in terms of health and are among the most important things for improving it. Yoga should be approached with an enthusiastic caution, not with fear and apprehension. Yoga, after all, is the only real solution to the sorrow and ignorance in which we live. As a process of returning to our own nature it is natural and spontaneous. The difficulty is in letting go of the ego — of the fears and desires we have erroneously regarded as who we really are. These complicate the practice of Yoga as they do all the things of life.

DRUGS

Most recreational drugs have a heating energy and increase Tejas. This includes psychedelic and hallucinogenic drugs (LSD, psilocybin, mescaline, marijuana etc.) that change our perception. Even common stimulants like coffee and tobacco (not regular tea, however) do this to some degree. Such drugs may afford some heightened perception by artificially stimulating Tejas, but they weaken our energy. First, since our nature is not purified, they may magnify our misconceptions. Second, they burn up Ojas very quickly. If Ojas is depleted below a certain threshold, it becomes difficult to build it up again. If people burn out their Ojas, they lose the capacity for real spiritual practice.

Drugs are Tamasic or dulling to the mind. Any short term stimulant, like an artificial shock, renders us more dull in the long run. Chemically produced drugs are toxic and lodge in the deeper tissues where they can cause permanent harm. All drugs tend to damage Ojas, even medicinal drugs, and so we should use them with caution.

For those who have adequate Ojas (which is usually stronger when we are young and have not yet depleted it) and who can take certain organic consciousness-promoting drugs with the proper guidance and in a sacred manner, a few such experiences may perhaps be useful. However, they are generally inferior to what can be accomplished with yogic practices and are not necessary.

Meditation is not like a drug experience, or an alternative way of creating one. It is a way of de-hypnotizing the mind, of removing it from all external conditioning influences, compared to which the ordinary state of consciousness is a state drugged by external influences and internal toxins. Yoga requires that we value the integrity of our own awareness and attention, and no longer look to the outside for something to occupy our minds. In order to practice Yoga we must not be seeking any form of entertainment or looking for any magic from the outside to make us feel better. Yoga requires working through the forms of our ignorance — boredom, loneliness, and suffering — not trying to avoid them. This is the greatest adventure, because it alone takes us to a real and lasting happiness and understanding.

ADDITIONAL MOVEMENTS OF PRANA, TEJAS AND OJAS

Prana, Tejas, and Ojas have additional movements, so that the system presented here must remain general. Though Prana, Tejas and Ojas have their prime sites in the subtle body, they have their actions on other chakras as well. Though Tejas has its site in the Root chakra, once developed it moves through all the chakras before settling in the heart, which is the ultimate abode of the flame of awareness. Similarly, though Ojas has its site in the head, once activated it descends through the entire body, becoming centered in the heart, which is the origin of Ojas. Though Prana is located in the heart, it permeates the entire body as our underlying energy. The ultimate goal is for all three energies to permeate our entire psycho-physical being from the inmost heart.

✳ ✳ ✳

We can now see how clearly related Ayurveda is with Yoga and how the energies of Ayurveda reflect in the subtle body and the mind. The integral nature of Vedic and Tantric science should thus be clear. It is important that we explore this science in a rational and experiential manner. Then we can come to a new yogic approach that includes all the power of the tradition but which is adapted to our circumstances today. For this work to proceed there must be further research on the traditions of Veda, Yoga, and Ayurveda, both by individuals and groups, not merely on an academic level but on the level of practice.

By the Grace of the Divine Mother and Yoga Shakti may this book help inspire others to take up this work!

APPENDICES

1
THE TEN WISDOM GODDESSES
AND BUDDHISM

The Goddess Speaks: Every place you see is my temple.
All events are acts of worship to me. At all times are my
holy celebrations, as I am the nature of all.
                                                    — *Devi Gita X.3*

Buddhism has its own tradition of Tantra which has been preserved mainly in Tibet, but can be found to some extent in all the lands where Mahayana Buddhism (Great Vehicle) has prevailed, including China and Japan. Tantric Buddhism has much in common with Hinduism as a whole. In fact, it appears to have more in common with Hinduism than it does with the Theravadin Buddhist traditions of Southeast Asia. Tantric Buddhism is characterized by ritual worship (puja), devotion to forms of the Gods and Goddesses (bhakti), Mantra Yoga, and an emphasis on Yoga techniques, which are seldom found in the southern Buddhism of Sri Lanka, Burma and Thailand, but which are fundamental to Hinduism. Other aspects of Hindu and Vedic culture like fire rituals (homa), Ayurvedic medicine, and Vedic astrology are part of the Buddhist tradition, particularly the Tibetan.

Buddhist like Hindu Tantra employs images of Goddesses and Yoginis (female powers of Yoga). In at least two instances (Tara and Chhinnamasta) the Buddhist figures have the same names or descriptions as the Hindu Wisdom Goddesses. Tantric Buddhism teaches the worship of Hindu Goddesses like Sarasvati and Lakshmi — who correspond to Matangi and Kamala of the Wisdom Goddesses — and Hindu Gods like Ganesh and Kubera. The important deity Mahakala of Tibetan Buddhism appears to be a variation of the Shiva-Mahakala of Hinduism. The main Buddhist deity or Bodhisattva, Avalokiteshvara, is portrayed in forms similar to either Shiva or Vishnu.

TARA

The Goddess Tara is perhaps the most obvious common deity in both Hindu and Buddhist traditions. In the Buddhist tradition Tara is the foremost of the female Bodhisattvas: a being who lived once and took a vow to help all beings in the future who call on her. The Buddhist Bodhisattvas have more or less the same role as the deities in the Hindu tradition. They are not simply great beings from the past, but cosmic principles and ultimately consciousness itself. In this regard Tara appears as the Buddhist form of the Supreme Goddess, Divine Mother, creator, preserver and destroyer of the worlds. Similarly, while the Hindu Goddess is the cosmic Mother beyond any need for creaturely incarnation, like a Bodhisattva she takes form to aid, teach or save living beings. She is ever present for us to call upon.

Tara in the Buddhist tradition occupies a role like Maheshvari or Mahadevi, the Great Goddess and Mother of the worlds in Hinduism. She stands for the feminine power generally and has many different forms. On the other hand, the figure of Tara in the Hindu tradition is not as commonly mentioned as deities like Lakshmi, Kali, Durga, Parvati, or Sarasvati. Tara is generally regarded as a form of Durga, who often stands for the Supreme Mother herself. As such Durga-Tara can be regarded as the supreme Goddess for both Hindus and Buddhists.

The word Tara is an ancient Sanskrit term. It first occurs in the *Yajur Veda* (an early text of the pre-Buddhist era) in the masculine tense as a name for Lord Shiva as the one who saves or delivers us from darkness and sorrow.

> *Reverence to the deliverer (Tara), reverence to the bestower of bliss and to bestower of delight, reverence to the maker of peace and to the maker of delight, reverence to the auspicious one (Shiva) and to the most auspicious one.*   — *Taittiriya Samhita IV.5.8*

The name Tara first occurs in the same section of the *Vedas* wherein the great mantra of reverence to Shiva (namaḥ Shivayā) also first occurs, and as one of the seven main names for this deity.

Tarini, which like Tara means the deliverer, is used as a name for Durga in the *Mahabharata*. It occurs in Arjuna's Hymn to Durga before the Mahabharata War in which he invokes her grace for victory in the battle. The main function of Durga is to deliver or save us from difficulty, just like Tara. The worship of Durga-Tara and of Shiva are part of the same tradition going back to Vedic times.

Both Buddhism and Hinduism employ the image of wisdom as being the ship that takes us across the waters of the world or the ocean of Samsara. Both wisdom and ship are feminine terms in Sanskrit. The Buddhist term for wisdom, Prajña, is a Vedic term and occurs in the

Upanishads as well, along with many other Vedic feminine terms for wisdom or the word (like medha, dhi, mati, manisha, vak, vani, nau).

A mantra to Durga, which occurs in the supplement to the *Rig Veda*, speaks of her saving action using the term Tara:

> *The twice-born who worship the beautiful, gentle God-dess who has the color of fire, the Fire takes them across (tarayati) all difficulties, as a ship across the sea.*
> — *Rig Veda Parishishthani 26.8*

The Sanskrit root tri, "to deliver," is common in Vedic thought, particularly in the metaphor of crossing the sea. Tara is the same in both Hinduism and Buddhism as a Goddess of wisdom and deliverance symbolized by the ship of the Divine Word, but she is more commonly called Durga in the Hindu tradition, wherein she has a greater variety of functions and aspects as the consort of Lord Shiva.

The rishi or seer for Hindu Tara is Akshobhya, who is her consort in Buddhist terminology and also a Bodhisattva. The Hindu Akshobhya is a form of Lord Shiva, who like the meaning of the term cannot be disturbed or shaken. In addition, Tara (or Nila Sarasvati as she is also called) is related to China or Mahachina, China or Tibet, in Hindu Tantric texts (like the *Devi Gita*). This connects the Hindu Tara with Buddhist influences. However, ancient Vedic and pre-Buddhist texts (like *Aitareya Brahmana viii. 14*) speak of Vedic lands located "beyond the Himalayas," suggesting that Tibet was earlier a land of Vedic culture. The pre-Buddhist Tibetan Bon religion, we note, contains many elements of Hindu and Vedic teachings like Shaivism.

The Buddhist meditation form of Tara is similar to the Hindu form of Lakshmi. Both are usually figured in the same seated pose, with the right leg hanging down, with two lotuses on either side, and having the same basic hand gestures. The only difference is that the Buddhist Tara makes the hand gestures touching the thumb and index finger, while Lakshmi has her hands open. The Hindu Tara has a form more like Kali, as discussed in her section of the book. This is because the Buddhist Tara as a general form of the Goddess contains many of the functions of the Divine Mother which in Hinduism are given to Lakshmi and Sarasvati.

Hence there is little difference between the form, function and usage of Tara in the Hindu and Buddhist traditions, or of the place of the Goddess as a whole and the ways of her worship. Some scholars, notably Lama Govinda, have attempted to differentiate Buddhist feminine Bodhisattvas from Hindu Goddesses under the idea that the former represent wisdom

(Prajña), while the latter represent only power (Shakti), which are said to be different concepts. This distinction is superficial, as should already be evident from the information in this book. Hindu Goddesses possess three forms as knowledge, power and beauty (the three basic forms of Sarasvati, Kali and Lakshmi), which always go together. Moreover, Shakti is Cit-Shakti, the power of consciousness. The Hindu Goddesses are also called Vidyas or forms of knowledge. And Buddhist Prajña has its power to enlighten, save or protect, and is similarly the source of love, compassion and beauty.

We are drawn to the following conclusion: The form of Tara that we find in the Hindu tradition appears to be in harmony with the development of the same name and term from ancient Vedic sources. The function of Tara as the deliverer, which is one aspect of Shiva's consort, does not require outside influence to explain its place within the Hindu tradition. Tara as a name for both Shiva and his consort can be traced to Vedic hymns long before the advent of the Buddha.

Buddhism develops the idea of saving wisdom which is inherent in Buddhist thought, through the form of Tara, who becomes its prime formulation of the role of the Goddess. This may be a development of the earlier Vedic idea of saving wisdom, or it may be an independent development. The feminine nature of wisdom does not appear to be limited to any particular tradition as we can observe through feminine figures such as Sophia of Gnosticism or Isis in ancient Egypt. Thus nothing in the Buddhist idea of Tara requires an outside influence to explain her role either.

This is not to say that the two forms of Tara are not related, but that their relationship is more owing to the general affinity between the two traditions than any specific borrowing. Both traditions reflect a common basis in Vedic culture, in the yogic tradition and in Tantra. While there have been differences between them, these have largely been superficial and semantic. The two traditions overlap to a great extent, which is what we see in their images of the Goddess. Just as terms like karma, dharma or nirvana occur commonly in both traditions because they share a common culture and language, so do forms of the Gods and Goddesses appear in each. The origin of the term Tara, however, derives from the *Vedas*, which predate Buddhism. Yet the emphasis on the name Tara as the supreme Goddess is primarily Buddhist.

Both Hinduism and Buddhism (and Jainism as well), we should note, follow the same rules for depicting icons, including their ornaments, weapons, apparel, stances and gestures (mudras), and for the methods of ritual worship, the use of mantras, yantras and other practices. If we examine the Buddhist mantra to Tara, it is similar to the mantras to Hindu Goddesses.

Om tāre tutāre ture svāhā!

The mantra begins with Om, which is the foremost of the Vedic mantras and also called Taraka or the power of deliverance. The mantra ends with Svāhā, the main mantra whereby offerings are made to Agni or the Vedic sacred fire, which is also regarded as another name for Durga. Tura means quickly; the Goddess is extolled for her speedy help to her devotees.

CHHINNAMASTA/ VAJRA YOGINI

The role of the Yoginis, or feminine deities of Yoga, occurs in both Hindu and Buddhist thought. In Buddhism the Yoginis, like the Bodhisatt-vas, are spirits who guide us in the practice of Yoga. The Yoginis appear in Hindu thought not just as guides of Yoga practice but as fierce Goddesses and forms of Kali.

The foremost of the Buddhist Yoginis is Vajra Yogini. She is related to Vajra Sattva (the diamond being), who is the main deity of the Vajrayana, the Vajra Path, which is said to be a higher path even than the Mahayana or Great Vehicle. The Buddhist depiction of Vajra Yogini is exactly the same as Chhinnamasta, a headless trunk holding her cut-off head in one hand and drinking her own blood. Hindu Chhinamasta is also called Vajra Vairochani, or the resplendent lady of the Vajra or thunder-bolt. The wielder of the Vajra in the *Vedas* is none other than Indra, the foremost of the old Vedic Gods. However, we should not confuse Vedic Indra with the Indra of later Hindu and Buddhist thought, who is merely the Lord of Heaven or the King of the Gods. Vedic Indra is the Supreme God who gives enlightenment. His main action is to win the Sun, the symbol of the Atman or Self-nature.

Indra found That Truth, the Sun that was dwelling in
darkness. — *Vishvamitra, RV III.39.5*

Hence the Buddhist worship of Vajra Yogini and Vajra Sattva appears to be a later form of the worship of the supreme Vedic God Indra and his consort.

GENERAL CONNECTIONS
BETWEEN HINDUISM AND BUDDHISM

Many other Hindu and Buddhist deities and practices are similar. The Buddhist tradition has a dark Goddess like Kali who wears a garland of skulls and is worshipped on a cremation ground. Hence though there are variations of name, form and function, all the main ideas behind the Dasha Mahavidya, as well as many of the Hindu Goddesses going back to the *Vedas*, have parallels in Buddhist thought, so much so that combining their forms of worship may be possible without any violation of their meaning.

While Hinduism and Buddhism may differ in terms of names and forms, their essential yogic practices are the same. Their semantic differences can generally easily be resolved, which issue we will examine briefly here, though it requires a study in its own right. Most important is the view that the Buddhist idea of anatman or non-ego is opposed to the Hindu concept of Atman or the higher Self.

While this dichotomy appears at first to be striking, if we look more deeply it disappears. The Hindu Atman or Self is not the ego or self-image, the conditioned entity identified with the body-mind complex (though Atman in a lower sense can have these meanings). The more common term for ego in Hindu thought is ahankara or the "I-fabrication." As Krishna states:

> *The wise man who abandoning all desires lives free of craving, who has no sense of ego (nirahankara) or of mineness (nirmama), attains to peace.*
> — *Bhagavad Gita II.71*

This concept, found also in Buddhist texts, is equally the essence of Buddhism and Hinduism.

While Buddhism does technically reject the term Atman, it has similar terms like "Self-nature" or "one's original face before birth." Terms like "pure consciousness," "non-duality" or the "absolute" are common in both traditions. The Buddhist term Bodhicitta, like the Hindu Atman, refers to the enlightened consciousness which dwells within the heart. Both traditions thus revolve around a discrimination between the ego (Buddhist atman or Hindu ahankara) and enlightened awareness (Buddhist Bodhichitta or Hindu Atman). Yet both traditions agree that truth transcends all words, ideas and dichotomies of the mind and is best revealed by silence or by the negation of all names and terms. In the *Brihadaranyaka*, the oldest *Upanishad*, Brahman (the Absolute) is described as "neti-neti" or not this, not that. This view is the same as the

Voidness teaching of Buddhism, Shunyavada, as emphasized by great Mahayana Buddhist teacher Nagarjuna, that truth is beyond all conceptual views.

Buddhism also appears to reject the term Brahman, the Godhead or Absolute of Hinduism. Yet it has similar terms like the unborn, uncreate, Absolute or Dharmakaya. In fact the Hindu equation that Atman is Brahman can be identified with the Buddhist equation Mind is Buddha. Atman and Mind stand for pure consciousness, not for the ego or conditioned mind. Buddha and Brahman stand for the supreme reality. Hence Hinduism and Buddhism are two formulations of the same yogic tradition, differing in approach but not in essence.

2
PRONUNCIATION OF SANSKRIT

I have placed only the mantras in transliterated Sanskrit to allow for their correct pronunciation. Other Sanskrit terms I have placed in their most common English equivalents (for which there is no standard model).

There are slight variations in Sanskrit pronunciation throughout India, as well as variations in the sounds that some letters correspond to. For example, v is sometimes pronounced w.

Those wishing to practice the mantras mentioned in the book should be taught them by one who knows them in order to get not only the correct pronunciation but the proper tone and rhythm of the chants.

16 VOWELS

a, as in b*u*t
ā, as in f*a*ther
i, as in s*i*t
n seat
u, as in p*u*t
ū, as in b*oo*t
e, as in m*a*de
ai, as in b*i*te
o, as in r*o*pe
au, as in f*ou*nd
ṛ, as in me*rri*ly
ṝ, as in ma*ri*ne
ḷ, as in reve*lry*
ḹ, same as above sound but longer vowel
am, nasalization of the vowel
aḥ, short aspirate or h-sound

25 CONSONANTS
5 GUTTURALS (with the throat)

k, as in *k*ept
kh, as in in*kh*orn
g, as in *g*o
gh, as in log*h*ouse

ṅ, as in ri*ng*

5 PALATALS (with the soft palate)

c, as in *ch*ip
ch, as it it*ch*
j, as in *j*udge
jh, as in he*dgeh*og
ñ, as in ca*ny*on

5 CEREBRALS
(with the tongue placed back toward the roof of the mouth)

ṭ, as in *t*rue
ṭh, as in nu*th*ook
ḍ, as in *d*rum
ḍh, as in re*dh*ead
ṇ, as in *n*one

5 DENTALS (with the tongue placed behind the teeth)

t, as in *t*ongue
th, as in an*th*ill
d, as in *d*ot
dh, as in a*dh*ere
n, as in *n*ot

5 LABIALS (with the lips)

p, as in *p*ick
ph, as in u*ph*ill
b, as in *b*oat
bh, as in a*bh*or
m, as in *m*other

9 SEMIVOWELS AND SIBILANTS

y, as in *y*es
r, as in *r*oad (rolling the r)
l, as in *l*ight
v, as in *v*ote
ś or sh, as in *s*ure
ṣ, as in *sh*ut
s, as in *s*it
h, as in *h*ead
kṣ, ksh

3
GLOSSARY OF
SANSKRIT TERMS

Advaita Vedanta	non-dualistic form of Vedanta
Agamas	Hindu scriptures after the Vedas
Agni	Vedic sacred fire
Agnihotra	Vedic fire offerings and invocations
Ahamkara	ego
Aim	mantra of wisdom and learning
Ajña Chakra	the third eye center
Akshobhya	A Bodhisattva or form of Shiva, he who cannot be shaken
Amrita Nadi	the immortal nadi
Anahata Chakra	heart or air chakra
Ananda	bliss
Anna	food
Apana Vayu	descending vital air
Apas	water
Artha	pursuit of wealth
Aryan	people of spiritual values
Asanas	yogic postures
Atharva Veda	fourth Veda
Atman	Divine or higher Self, pure consciousness
Atma vichara	Self-inquiry
Avalokiteshvara	Buddhist deity of saving grace and wisdom
Avidya	ignorance
Ayurveda	Vedic Medicine
Bagala	Bagalamukhi
Bala	Sundari as a child Goddess
Bandhas	yogic locks
Bhagavad Gita	scripture of the avatar Krishna
Bhairava	Shiva in his terrible or wrathful form
Bhairavi	the Goddess in her terrible or wrathful form
Bhakti Yoga	Yoga of Devotion

Bhasma	ash or oxide preparation
Bhuvaneshvari	the Goddess as the ruler of the universe
Bindu	point or drop: the point of pure awareness in which time and space collapse into a single point
Brahmacharya	control of sexual energy; state of life of learning and purity
Brahma	form of the Hindu trinity governing creation
Brahman	the Absolute or ultimate reality
Brahmanas	Vedic ritualistic texts
Buddha	ninth avatar of Vishnu
Buddhism	non-orthodox form of Vedic\Aryan teaching based on the teachings of Lord Buddha or enlightened one
Buddhi	intelligence or discriminating faculty
Chakras	nerve centers of the subtle body
Chamunda	wrathful form of Kali
Chandi	wrathful form of Kali
Chhinnamasta	the form of the Goddess as without a head
Cit	consciousness
Citta	field of consciousness
Dakini	Yogini or female attendant deity
Dakshinachara	right-handed path in Tantra
Dakshina Kali	wisdom aspect of Kali
Dakshinamurti	Shiva as the giver of knowledge, seer of Shri Chakra
Dasha Mahavidya	Ten Great Wisdom Forms of the Goddess
Deva	God, deity, cosmic power
Devi	Goddess, deity, cosmic power
Dharana	yogic concentration or attention
Dharma	teaching or religion; honor or status
Dhatus	seven bodily tissues in Ayurvedic Medicine
Dhumavati	The smoke form of the Goddess as the grandmother
Dhyana	meditation
Doshas	biological humors of Ayurvedic medicine
Durga	the Goddess as the destroyer of demons
Ganapati/Ganesha	elephant faced God who destroys all obstacles
Gauri	form of Parvati
Gayatri	Vedic chant for awakening the soul
Grihastha	householder stage of life
Gunas	prime qualities of nature
Guru	spiritual teacher

Hanuman	the monkey God, symbol of Prana
Hatha Yoga	Yoga of the physical body
Havana	same as Homa
Hinduism	modern name for the Vedic teaching
Homa	Vedic worship, Fire offerings
Hrim	great mantra of the Goddess
Hum	great mantra of Agni and Shiva
Ida Nadi	left or lunar channel of the subtle body
Indra	Vedic God of being, life and perception
Ishvara	the cosmic Creator
Jainism	non-orthodox form of Vedic/Aryan teaching emphasizing non-violence
Jñana Yoga	Yoga of Knowledge
Jyeshta	another name for Dhumavati
Jyotish	Vedic Astrology
Kailas	the world mountain
Kali, Kalika	the dark form of the Goddess, the Goddess as power of death and transformation
Kali Yuga	dark or iron age
Kama	pursuit of desire
Kamala/ Kamalatmika	Goddess of the Lotus
Kapha	biological water humor
Karma	Law of Cause and Effect
Karma Yoga	Yoga of Work or Service
Kashmir Shaivism	Shaivite philosophy of medieval Kashmir
Kaula	unorthodox Tantric path
Kaya Kalpa	Ayurvedic therapy for complete physical rejuvenation
Ketu	south node of the Moon
Kirtana	devotional singing
Klim	mantra of love and devotion
Krim	mantra of action and transformation
Krishna	eighth avatar of Vishnu
Kriya	the power of action
Kriya Yoga	yoga of technique
Kshatriya	people of political values
Kula	family or group
Kundalini	serpent power

Lakshmi	Goddess of prosperity and beauty; consort of Vishnu
Lalita	Goddess of the bliss of spiritual knowledge
Laya Yoga	Yoga of absorption into the sound-current (nada)
Linga	pillar-like symbol of Shiva or cosmic masculine force
Mada	use of wine or intoxicants
Madhyama	the middle stage of speech or mental speech
Mahabharata	epic story of Krishna and the Pandavas
Mahadeva	the Great God
Mahadevi	the Great Goddess
Mahakala	the great form of Kala
Mahakali	the great form of Kali
Maheshvari	the Goddess as the great ruler of the universe
Mahalakshmi	the great form of Lakshmi
Mahasarasvati	the great form of Saraswati
Mahayana	great vehicle
Mahishasura Mardini	Durga as the destroyer of Mahishasura, the bull symbolizing vital passions
Maithuna	sexual intercourse
Mamsa	meat
Manas	mind or emotion
Manipura Chakra	fire or navel center
Mantra	spiritual or empowered speech
Mantrini	Goddess as counselor
Manu	Vedic original man
Matangi	Goddess of energize speech and music
Matsya	fish
Maya	illusion
Mayavada	doctrine that the world is unreal
Meru	the world mountain
Moksha	liberation
Mudra	hand gestures, also means money or wealth
Nada	sound current
Nadis	nerves or channels of the subtle body
Nataraj	Shiva as lord of the cosmic dance
Nirvana	liberation, the state of peace
Ojas	primary energy reserve of the body
Om	mantra of the Divine

Pancha Karma	Ayurvedic purification therapy consisting of use of emetics, purgatives, enemas and nasal medications
Para	supreme state of speech as Silence
Parvati	consort of Shiva as the daughter of the mountain
Pashyanti	illumined speech
Patañjali	main teacher of classical Yoga system
Phat	mantra of power and protection
Pingala	right or solar channel of the subtle body
Pitta	biological fire humor
Prachanda Chandi	the fierce form of Chandi
Prajña	wisdom as the Goddess
Prakriti	great Nature, matter
Prana	breath or life-force
Pranayama	yogic control of the breath
Pratyahara	yogic control of mind and senses
Praval	coral
Puja	Hindu worship
Puranas	Hindu religious and mythological texts
Purusha	pure consciousness, spirit
Radha	consort of Krishna
Rahu	north node of the Moon; dragon's head
Rajarajeshvari	the Goddess as the Supreme Queen of the universe
Rajas	quality of energy or agitation
Raja Yoga	integral or royal yoga path of Patanjali
Rama	seventh avatar of Vishnu
Ramayana	epic story of Rama
Rasayana	Ayurvedic rejuvenation methods
Rig Veda	oldest Hindu scripture; Veda of chant
Rishis	ancient Vedic seers
Rudra	terrible or wrathful form of Shiva
Sacchidananda	Being-Consciousness-Bliss
Sahasranama	thousand names
Sahasra Padma	thousand-petalled lotus or head chakra
Sama Veda	Veda of song
Samadhi	absorption
Samana Vayu	balancing vital air
Samaya	orthodox Tantric path
Samsara	realm of illusion, opposite Nirvana
Sankhya	Vedic philosophy of cosmic principles

Sanskrit	Vedic and mantric language
Sannyasa	stage of life of renunciation and liberation
Sanatana Dharma	the eternal teaching; traditional name for the Hindu religion
Sarasvati	Goddess of speech, learning, knowledge and wisdom
Sat	being
Sattva	quality of truth or light
Savitar	Vedic Sun god as the guide of Yoga
Seva	service
Shakti	the power of consciousness and spiritual evolution
Shankaracharya	the great philosopher of non-dualistic Vedanta
Shiva	form of the Hindu trinity governing destruction and transcendence
Siddhas	perfected beings
Sikhs	Indian spiritual tradition since the fifteenth century
Skanda	second son of Shiva and Parvati
Sita	consort of Rama
So'ham	natural mantric sound of the breath
Soma	Vedic God of bliss
Shri Chakra	foremost of the yantras
Srim	mantra of Lakshmi and of the Goddess in general
Shri Vidya	the knowledge or teaching relative to the Shri Chakra
Stambhana	stopping or paralyzing action
Sundari	Goddess of beauty and bliss
Sunya	the void or emptiness
Surya	Vedic Sun God or deity of the enlightened mind
Sushumna	central channel or nadi of the subtle body
Svadhishthana	sex or water chakra
Svaha	mantra of consecration
Tamas	quality of darkness and inertia
Tantras	medieval yogic and ritualistic teachings
Tara	the Goddess in her role as savioress
Tejas	radiance, the subtle form of Pitta or fire
Trataka	Yogic practice of steady gazing
Tripura	three cities or states of waking, dream and deep sleep
Tripura Bhairavi	the triple form of Bhairavi
Tripura Sundari	the triple form of Sundari

Udana Vayu	ascending vital air
Uma	The Goddess as Shiva's consort as the giver of knowledge
Upanishads	Vedic philosophical texts
Upasana	worship, including meditation
Vaikhari	coarse or audible speech
Vak	Speech or Divine Word as the Goddess
Vajra	lightning or thunderbolt as the weapon of enlightenment
Vajra Yogini	the lightning or diamond Yogini, Chhinnamasta
Vamachara	left-handed path in Tantra
Vata	biological air humor
Vayu	wind
Vedas	ancient scriptures of India
Vedanta	Vedic philosophy of Self-knowledge
Vedic Science	integral spiritual science of the *Vedas*
Vichara	inquiry
Vidya	knowledge or wisdom, the Goddess
Vijñana	intelligence
Vishnu	form of the Hindu trinity governing preservation
Vishuddha	throat or ether chakra
Viveka	discrimination
Vyana Vayu	diffusive vital air
Yajña	sacrifice
Yajur Veda	Veda of ritual or sacrifice
Yantra	geometrical meditation designs
Yoga	techniques of developing and integrating energy
Yoga Shakti	the power of yoga as a force of the Goddess
Yoga Sutras	classical text of the sage Patañjali on Yoga
Yogi	practitioner of yoga
Yogini	female yogi, female yogic power or attendant deity
Yoni	ring like symbol of Shakti or cosmic feminine power
Yugas	world-ages

4
GLOSSARY OF
SPECIAL ORIENTAL HERBS

amalaki	Emblica officinalis
ashwagandha	Withania somnifera
bala	Sida cordifolia
bibhitaki	Terminalia baelerica
brahmi	Centella or Hydrocotyle asiatica
champak	Michelia champaca
pippali	Piper longum
dang gui	Angelica sinense
haritaki	Terminalia chebula
heena	Lawsonia alba
he shou wu	Polygonum multiflorum
khus	Andropogon muricatus
lycium berries	Lycium sinense
manduka parni	Bacopa monniera
rehmannia	Rehmannia glutinosa
shatavari	Asparagus racemosus
tulsi	Ocinum sanctum
vidari	Ipomeia digitata

5
BIBLIOGRAPHY

ENGLISH

Abhinavagupta. *Paratrisika Vivarana* (trans. Jaideva Singh). Delhi, India: Motilal Banarsidass, 1988.

Candi Path (Devi Mahatmyam, trans. by Swami Satyananda Saraswati). Martinez, California: Devi Mandir, 1985.

Caraka Samhita (three volumes). Varanasi, India: Chowkhamba Sanskrit Series.

Devi Gita (trans. by Swami Satyananda Saraswati). Martinez, California: Devi Mandir, 1985.

Devi Mahatmyam. Madras, India: Sri Ramakrishna Math, 1974.

Frawley, David. *Astrology of the Seers*. Salt Lake City, Utah: Passage Press, 1990.

Frawley, David. *Ayurvedic Healing*. Salt Lake City, Utah: Passage Press, 1989.

Frawley, David. *Beyond the Mind*. Salt Lake City, Utah: Passage Press, 1992.

Frawley, David. From the *River of Heaven: Hindu and Vedic Knowledge for the Modern Age*. Salt Lake City, Utah: Passage Press, 1990.

Frawley, David. *Gods, Sages and Kings: Vedic Secrets of Ancient Civilization*. Salt Lake City, Utah: Passage Press, 1991.

Frawley, David. *Wisdom of the Ancient Seers: Selected Mantras from the Rig Veda*. Salt Lake City, Utah: Passage Press, 1991.

Frawley, David and Vasant Lad. *The Yoga of Herbs*. Santa Fe, New Mexico: Lotus Press, 1986.

Ganapati Muni, Vasishtha. *Epistles of Light*. Madras, India: Kavyakantha Vasishtha Ganapati Muni Trust, 1978.

Johari, Haresh. *Tools for Tantra*. Rochester, Vermont: Inner Traditions International, 1986.

Krishna, G. *Nayana*. Madras, India: Kavyakantha Vasishtha Ganapati Muni Trust, 1978.

Lad, Vasant Dr. *Ayurveda, The Science of Self-healing*. Santa Fe, New Mexico: Lotus Press, 1984.

Lalita Sahasranama. Madras, India: The Theosophical Publishing House, 1976.

Pandit, M.P. *Adoration of the Divine Mother.* Madras, India: Ganesh and Company, 1973.

Rao, Prof. S.K. Ramachandra. *The Tantrik Practices in Sri Vidya.* Bangalore, India: Kalpatharu Research Academy Publication, 1990.

Rao, Prof. S.K. Ramachandra, *Pratima Kosha* (in four volumes). Bangalore, India: Kalpatharu Research Academy Publication.

Satguru Sivaya Subramuniyaswami. *Dancing with Shiva.* India and USA: Himalayan Academy, 1993.

Satyeswarananda Giri, Swami. *Inner Victory.* San Diego, California: Sanskrit Classics, 1987.

Shankaracharya. *Saundaryalahari* (V.K. Subramanian trans.). Delhi, India: Motilal Banarsidass, 1986.

Shankaranarayan, S. *Bhagavan and Nayana.* Tiruvannamalai, India: Sri Ramanasramam, 1983.

Shankaranarayan, S. *The Ten Great Cosmic Powers.* Pondicherry, India: Dipti Publications, 1975.

Shankaranarayan, S. *Sri Chakra.* Pondicherry, India: Dipti Publications, 1978.

Yogeshwarananda Saraswati, Swami. *Science of Soul.* New Delhi, India: Yoga Niketan Trust, 1987

SANSKRIT

Abhinavagupta. *Tantrasara.* Delhi, India: Bani Prakashan, 1983.

Atharva Veda. Ajmer, India: Srimati Paropakarini Sabhaya, 1976.

Brhatstotra Ratnakara. Bombay, India: Keshava Bhikaji Davale, 1986.

Srimad Devibhagavatam. Varanasi, India: Chawkhamba, 1989.

Ganapati Muni, Vasishtha. *Adivedasya Bhasyadigrantha.* Vijayanagar, India: Madhukeswara Rao, 1971.

Ganapati Muni, Vasishtha. *Gitamala.* Sirsi, North Kanara, India: D.S. Vishwamitra, 1959.

Ganapati Muni, *Umasahasradigranthasangraha.* Vijayanagar, India: Madhukeswara Rao.

Ganapati Muni, *Mahavidyadi Sutrgaranthavali.* Yellamanchili, India: G.L. Kantam. 1958.

Ganapati Muni, *Mahavidyasutradi Sangraha.* Vijayanagar, India: Madhukeswara Rao, 1972.

Ganapati Muni, *Mahavidyadi Sutras.* Vizianagram, India: Madhukeswara Rao, 1969.

Mahabharata (in four volumes). Gorakhpur, India: Gita Press.

Mantra Pushpa. Bombay, India: Ramakrishna Math, Khar, Bombay, 1990.

Mishra, Mukundavallabha. *Karmathaguru.* Delhi, India: Motilal Banarsidass, 1976.

Patañjali, *Yoga Sutras.* Varanasi, India: Bharatiya Vidya Prakashana.

Rig Veda. Bombay, India: Svadhyaya Mandala.

Shastri, Kapali, *Collected Works Volume Seven, Uma Sahasram.* Pondicherry, India: Dipti Publications, 1987.

Shastri, Kapali, *Collected Works Volume Nine, Sanskrit Writings* 2. Pondicherry, India: Dipti Publications, 1990.

Shiva Maha Purana. Delhi, India: Nag Publications, 1981.

Taittiriya Aranyaka. Delhi, India: Motilal Banarsidass, 1985.

Upanishads, One Hundred and Eighty Eight. Delhi, India: Motilal Banarsidass, 1980.

Yajur Veda (Vajasaneya Samhita). Bombay, India: Svadhyaya Mandala, 1970.

General Index

Herbs and Remedies Index

David Frawley and K. Natsan

BIODATA

David Frawley (Vamadeva Shastri) is one of the few Westerners recognized in India as a Vedacharya or teacher of the ancient Vedic wisdom. He is the author of numerous books and articles on Vedic topics including Ayurveda, Vedic Astrology, Vedanta, Hinduism, Yoga and Tantra, as well as translations and interpretations from the Vedas.

Dr. Frawley as been given many awards for his work in India including the Veda Vyasa award by the International Institute of Indian Studies. He is a Jyotish Kovid through the Indian Council of Astrological Sciences, and is also the President of the American Council of Vedic Astrology, the American offshoot of the Indian Council. He has a Doctor's degree in Chinese Medicine and has also been certified as an expert through the University of Poona for his knowledge of Yoga and Ayurveda. He is presently director of the American Institute of Vedic Studies.

AYURVEDIC CORRESPONDENCE COURSE

Ayurveda is the traditional natural healing system of India and one of the most holistic forms of medicine in the world. This course of five hundred pages, based upon the book *Ayurvedic Healing,* covers all the main aspects of Ayurvedic medicine in order to give the student the foundation to practice this ancient healing art.

PART I consists of Introduction, the Background of Ayurveda through Yoga Philosophy, and an in depth examination of Ayurvedic Anatomy and Physiology (Doshas, Dhatus, Malas, Srotas, Kalas and Organs).

PART II is Constitutional Analysis, Mental nature, the Disease Process, Diagnosis (including pulse), Patient Examination, Yoga and Ayurvedic Psychology.

PART III is Therapy includes Dietary and Herbal Therapy in depth, Therapeutic Methods (including Pancha Karma), Subtle Healing Modalities (gems, colors, aromas and mantras), and Practical Application of Yoga Psychology.

Special Health Care Professional's Version of Course includes advanced material on Herbal Treatment through the Channel Systems, Marma Points, and the Science of Prana.

The course is affiliated with Ashtanga Ayurvedic College in Pune, India and with the Hindu University of America. Certification is granted upon completion, as well as options for further study.

VEDIC ASTROLOGY CORRESPONDENCE COURSE

Vedic (Hindu) Astrology or Jyotish, is the traditional astrology of India, used along with Yoga and Ayurveda. This course of five hundred pages, based on the book *The Astrology of the Seers,* teaches the primary principles of Vedic Astrology and shows the student how to give a Vedic Astrology reading. Topics include Planets, Signs, Houses, Aspects, Yogas, Harmonic Charts, Planetary Periods (dasas and bhuktis), Nakshatras, Ashtakavarga, Horary and Electional Astrology (muhurta). Additional topics of Relationship Astrology, Business Astrology, and principles of chart interpretation are examined.

The course also explains the Astrology of Healing including the use of gems, mantras, yantras, and deities to help balance planetary influences and goes into detail in regard to Medical Astrology (Ayurveda), Karmic Astrology and Spiritual Astrology.

The course presents the Vedic system in clear, practical and modern terms and as adapted to Western culture. Certification is given upon course completion along with options for further study both through the American Council of Vedic Astrology and the Indian Council of Astrological Sciences.

For information on courses send a self-addressed stamped envelope to:

AMERICAN INSTITUTE OF VEDIC STUDIES
P.O. BOX 8357, SANTA FE, NM 87504-8357

BOOKS OF RELATED INTEREST

The Astrology of the Seers
A Guide to Vedic Astrology by David Frawley
    ISBN 1-878423-05-3   342 pp. $18.95

Ayurvedic Healing
A Comprehensive Guide by David Frawley
    ISBN 1-878423-05-3   342 pp. $18.95

Beyond the Mind
    ISBN 1-878423-14-2   173 pp. $12.95

From the River of Heaven
Hindu and Vedic Knowledge for the Modern Age by David Frawley
    ISBN 1-878423-01-1   180 pp. $12.95

Gods, Sages and Kings
Vedic Secrets of Ancient Civilization by David Frawley
    ISBN 1-878423-08-8   396 pp. $19.95

Wisdom of the Ancient Seers
Mantras of the *Rig Veda* by David Frawley
    ISBN 1-878423-16-9   260 pp. $14.95

Myths and Symbols of Vedic Astrology by Bepin Behari
    ISBN 1-878423-06-1   278 pp. $14.95

Fundamentals of Vedic Astrology
Vedic Astrologer's Handbook, Volume I by Bepin Behari
    ISBN 1-878423-09-6   280 pp. $14.95

Planets in the Signs and Houses
Vedic Astrologer's Handbook, Volume II by Bepin Behari
    ISBN 1-878423-10-X   258 pp. $14.95

Aspects in Vedic Astrology
by Pandit Gopesh Kumar Ojha and Pandit Ashutosh Ojha
    ISBN 1-878423-15-0   181 pp. $13.95

Astrological Healing Gems by Shivaji Bhattacharjee
    ISBN 1-878423-07-X   128 pp. $7.95

Natural Healing Through Ayurveda
by Dr. Subhash Ranade
    ISBN 1-878423-13-4   195 pp. $12.95

Interacting With Society
Life Strategies Series by Edward F. Tarabilda
    ISBN 1-878423-03-7   176 pp. $7.95

The Spiritual Quest
Life Strategies Series by Edward F. Tarabilda
    ISBN 1-87842 3-04-5   125 pp. $7.95